THE DEEPER THINGS OF GOD

UNLOCKING THE SECRETS OF GOD'S WORD

BY: VIRGIL ADAMS III

ISBN: 979-8337703015

Cover design by: Virgil Adams III

Library of Congress Control Number: 2018675309

Printed in the United States of America

Table of Contents

CHAPTER 0 (P.7) - BEFORE WE BEGIN

CHAPTER 1 (P.11) - THE BEGINNING

CHAPTER 2 (P.25) - THE TRINITY

CHAPTER 3 (P.43) - KINGDOM OF GOD AND
the KINGDOM OF HEAVEN

CHAPTER 4 (P.57) - THE OLD TESTAMENT

CHAPTER 5 (P.71) - CHRIST AND THE CHURCH

CHAPTER 6 (P.93) - THE MILLENNIAL REIGN &
THE END OF THE WORLD

CHAPTER 7 (P.109) - NEW HEAVEN AND EARTH

CHAPTER 8 (P.115) - WHAT IS LOVE?

CHAPTER 9 (P.125) - SUFFERING

CHAPTER 10 (P.143) - THE POWER OF THE CHRISTIAN

Chapter 0
Before We Begin

1 Corinthians 2:10-11(ESV)

For the Spirit searches all things, yes, the deep things of God. For what man knows the things of a man except the spirit of the man which is in him? Even so, no one knows the things of God except the Spirit of God.

Can God be comprehended; can we know the depths of His mind or the working of His hands? Simply answered, yes, but only when He chooses to reveal His mysteries to us. God's vast presence, power, and abilities are far beyond our understanding. Yet, He desires such a close relationship with us that He has made much known to us about Himself. In this book, we will go deeper into the revelations of God than we ever have before. Being able to understand the mysteries, histories, and insights of who God is, what He has done in this world, and what He has revealed about what He is going to do in the future. We will only use the Bible (God's 66 Canonical books) and will let the Bible define itself.

Throughout my whole life, there always seemed to be holes in my understanding of the Word. I asked God to give me an understanding of things about His word that would take the whole Bible and let it all flow together without errors or contradictions. As I was growing up, it seemed as if the Bible seemed to contradict itself many times. I wanted to understand why. Parts of the Bible that, if I held to my current understanding, I would have to ignore other parts of the Bible. For example, if there is no sin in heaven and we are safe after judgment (1 Thessalonians 4:17), not worrying about messing up and being cast into hell, then how did the angels do just that? I was not content in my spirit and began earnestly praying and seeking the truth. In this search, God has given me some new revelations. Taking the Bible as a whole, God began to put everything together without errancy or contradictions. The Bible began to be a giant puzzle. It pieced together perfectly without missing pieces or leaving extra verses that would not fit into it. We will cover history from the beginning to the end and then beyond. We have been missing so much in the Bible, but now it's time to bring these things to light. This personal journey of seeking truth has been transformative, and I hope it will inspire you in your own journey.

AN IMPORTANT WARNING!

This book is not intended for people without a foundation in Christianity. When you start your walk with God, you must be on milk. Learning the basics and taking each step in general knowledge. You will need to learn what the Bible says and why we must let it be the absolute authority in our lives. This book is intended for the seasoned Christians seeking answers to those questions that you never seemed to be able to get an answer for. Why did God plant a tree of knowledge if He knew they would fall? What happens to people who never knew God? Why does God allow suffering? How can the Trinity be understood? There are many more questions we will cover. This is not intended to be an apologetic book but rather a book for Christian growth in knowledge from a brother in Christ. This book starts with the presupposition that the Word of God is God's perfect message to His people so that we can know Him personally. That God is real and ready to be in a relationship with us. Who sent His one and only Son, Jesus Christ, who is part of the trinitarian Godhead, to redeem us from death to life, and by the drawing of the Holy Spirit, we can be saved and ready to spend eternity with Him forever.

Most, or maybe all, of what is in this book will challenge what you have thought about the Bible. It may be different from your current beliefs; If you disagree with it, I encourage you to prove it wrong by using the Bible alone. Don't go to commentaries or proceed with an argument from a human authority. Seek out the scriptures and reason from that alone. It should be a rule of thumb on all things, but you should never believe what you hear or read without seeking scripture. I encourage you not to believe anything you read in this book without seeking out if it is in line with God's Word. Whether it is from your pastor, evangelist, scholar, or friend. You should be like the Bereans in Acts 17.

"These (Berea) were more noble than those in Thessalonica in that they received the word with all readiness of mind and searched the scriptures daily whether those things were so." (KJV)

Keep your mind open to learning new things and being taught new things, but always with a mind of caution. Make sure it aligns with scripture before you accept it into your heart. Some of this will be hard to hear and definitely hard to accept. However, if you find it true, I plead with you to be ready to accept it and share it.

Chapter 1

The Beginning

If we are going to challenge your thinking, where do we start? Let's start in the same place I started. "In the beginning," with the question of why God allowed or even wanted Adam to fall. If God knew Adam would sin in the garden, and God did it anyway, how would that be any different than digging a hole in front of someone riding a bike and putting a tarp over it so they fall in along the way? This is an argument atheist have used against believers for a long time, and if that is the case, then they would be right. However, the truth is far different than what has been portrayed. There are a few questions you must ask yourself.

*Why did God put the trees (plural) in the garden?

*Why did God create the earth?

*How did God create the earth?

*What was before and after the earth?

The common question is why God planted the Tree of Knowledge when He knew it would make them fall. Conversely, we forget that there are two very different trees—a Tree of Life and a Tree of Knowledge of Good and Evil. In this, there is a more profound question no one seems to be asking: why did God make the Tree of Life in the first place? We always hear people asking why God created the Tree of Knowledge, but rarely do we ask why He made the Tree of Life. This answer is not hidden from us because God tells us clearly what the tree is for.

Then the LORD God said, "Behold, the man has become like one of Us, to know good and evil. And now, lest he put out his hand and take also of the tree of life, and eat, and live forever"— Genesis 3:22 (KJV)

In the midst of the street of it, and on either side of the river, was there the tree of life, which bare twelve manner of fruits, and yielded her fruit every month: and the leaves of the tree were for the healing of the nations. - Revelations 22:2 (KJV)

With the information given to us through the Bible, we see the Tree of Life was intended to let man eat its fruit and live forever or greatly extend their life. We are not told if man had to eat of it once or periodically to live forever. The most logical conclusion would be that the fruit would stop them from aging for a time, and then they could choose to eat it again or begin to age. Also, the leaves were to heal a person. Everything God made is made with purpose because God is the intelligent designer of everything. The tree is made to extend a person's life forever, which begs the question: What happens if they choose not to eat? Answer: They would not live forever. That would mean that Adam and Eve were not eternal beings from the start. This raises another question: If they ate the fruit, would they be able to die at all? The simplistic answer to all of this is that God always intended for their flesh to pass away from this earth. That might be new information to many, so let's back it up with some details.

Ask yourself what the consequence would be if Adam and Eve had never died. It would mean they would be eternally separated from God the Father. They would essentially be trapped on Earth for all eternity. God the Father dwells in the 3rd heaven, not on Earth; those on earth have never got to see or spend time with the Father. The Son and the Holy Spirit are on Earth and dwell with us. This means we will still be with God, but not the Father. The Garden of Eden was the specific home of the Son, His dwelling place. This is because the part of the Godhead, which is God the Father, has never been with man face to face. The Creator of the heavens, the earth, the sun, the moon, stars, animals, and who made man and put him in the garden was the Son (Jesus) and not the Father directly. This is clearly seen in a few places.

Genesis Ch 1-3 – In the beginning God created the heaven and the earth......

John 1:1-3 (ESV) - In the beginning was the Word, and the Word was with God, and the Word was God. The same was in the beginning with God. All things were made by him; and without him was not anything made that was made.

Colossians 1:15-20 (ESV) - He is the image of the invisible God, the firstborn over all creation. For by Him all things were created that are in heaven and that are on earth, visible and invisible, whether thrones or dominions or principalities or powers. All things were created through Him and for Him. And He is before all things, and in Him all things consist. And He is the head of the body, the church, who is the beginning, the firstborn from the dead, that in all things He may have the preeminence. For it pleased the Father that in Him all the fullness should dwell, and by Him to reconcile all things to Himself, by Him, whether things on earth or things in heaven, having made peace through the blood of His cross.

This verse shows that Jesus, the Son and God, is the creator of all things. The Son made our world and the universe. The one who walked with Adam and Eve from the time He created them and began teaching them. In Genesis Ch 2-3, we see God interacting with man, yet no man has ever seen the Father.

not that anyone has seen the Father except he who is from God; he has seen the Father. - John 6:46 (ESV)

Adam and Eve never physically saw the Father but were with God the Son. Just as we have not seen the Father, yet we spend each day with Him ourselves. Even if it were possible to somehow become immortal in this life, it would only hinder our primary purpose of making it to our home. Earth is not our home (Philippians 3:20). Our true home is to be with the Father who is in heaven. Even from the very beginning, man's purpose was to love God and live for Him during our lives. To obey and receive eternal favor with God, to leave this world behind, and to be with the Father

John 14:1-3 (ESV) - "Do not let your hearts be troubled. You believe in God; believe also in me. My Father's house has many rooms; if that were not so, would I have told you that I am going there to prepare a place for you? And if I go and prepare a place for you, I will come back and take you to be with me that you also may be where I am."

John 14:6 (ESV) - Jesus said to him, "I am the way and the truth and the life. No one comes to the Father except through me."

Here is another consequence to think about. If Adam and Eve lived forever on this earth, they would live in a perpetual existence of being able to fail, die, and then be separated from God forever. I said earlier that the logical conclusion to the Tree of Life fruit being a temporary stop to the aging process is because if it were a permanent stop to their age and making them immortal, they would be in the same situation. They could eat it regularly and live forever or choose not to eat, grow old, and go home to the Father. We know that death for the Christians is a finish line, that once crossed, we secure our rest in the Lord forever. death is not feared but celebrated. However, if Adam and Eve never got to celebrate this, their eternal existence would be a game of time asking themselves not if but when they would mess up and go to hell. Maybe it would be 100 years, maybe 100,000,000 years, but if it only took one bite and you had an eternity to take that bite, how long could you last? If this were true, this would be an evil game for God to play.

There were some that the Bible records who finished their goal and never had to taste death, Namely Enoch and Elijah. I'm not arguing here what these two may do later in their service to God. Only that God pulled them off the Earth because their ministry and time of testing were completed. This is not God having them live forever on Earth, but rather bringing them to the Father's house to rest with Him forever. They crossed the finish line without dying. We look forward to doing this ourselves one day when Jesus returns for His Church.

There is also a final point to this that I'd like to add, and it has to do with the reality of what the presence of the Father will do to physical matter. We know that the Father's face will not be seen by man until the last day, the day of the Great White Throne Judgment. When Jesus hands over the Kingdom of Heaven to the Father (1 Corinthians 15:24), the Father will come into our physical universe, and the overwhelming presence will utterly melt away all physical existence.

2 Peter 3:11-12 (ESV) - Since all these things are thus to be dissolved, what sort of people ought you to be in lives of holiness and godliness, waiting for and hastening the coming of the day of God, because of which the heavens will be set on fire and dissolved, and the heavenly bodies will melt as they burn!

Revelation 20:11 (ESV) - Then I saw a great white throne and him who was seated on it. From his presence, earth and sky fled away, and no place was found for them.

The sheer raw power of God's presence is so overpowering that physical elements cannot handle being in it. This is why God's Trinity is so important. If God the Father were to inhabit our physical space, it would be like trying to contain the power of our sun's core within our stomach. We need to understand that since the earth itself cannot stand in His presence, there was only the Son and Holy Spirit in the garden. Hence, for us to be able to spend eternity with the Father, we must first put off this earthly form. Our souls will take on a holy spiritual body that He will give us. That way, we can stand and be ready to spend eternity with Him. If Adam and Eve were eternally flesh, they would never be able to stand in the Father's presence.

This leads us to another important question: what was the death they received for eating the fruit?

But of the tree of the knowledge of good and evil, thou shalt not eat of it: for in the day that thou eatest thereof, thou shalt surely die. – Genesis 2:17 (KJV)

Romans gives us a direct answer to this question.

Romans 5:12-17 (ESV) - Therefore, just as sin came into the world through one man, and death through sin, and so death spread to all men because all sinned— for sin indeed was in the world before the law was given, but sin is not counted where there is no law. Yet death reigned from Adam to Moses, even over those whose sinning was not like the transgression of Adam, who was a type of the one who was to come. But the free gift is not like the trespass. For if many died through one man's trespass, much more have the grace of God and the free gift by the grace of that one man Jesus Christ abounded for many. And the free gift is not like the result of that one man's sin. For the judgment following one trespass brought condemnation, but the free gift following many trespasses brought justification. For if, because of one man's trespass, death reigned through that one man, much more will those who receive the abundance of grace and the free gift of righteousness reign in life through the one man Jesus Christ.

The death was immediate, for the day they ate, they would die. Their death was not physical but spiritual. Romans 5 gives us the best details and tells us that Jesus' sacrifice removed the punishment for sin, which wages will be our spiritual death.

Romans 5:21 (ESV) so that, as sin reigned in death, grace also might reign through righteousness leading to eternal life through Jesus Christ our Lord.

If it were a physical death, then those who turn to Christ would no longer physically die since the death sentence is negated by Christ's work. Since Christians still grow old and die, only a spiritual death can account for the death that Adam and Eve experienced as well.

With this understanding, let's examine the original question: Why did God plant the trees? They were given full permission to use the Tree of Life and enjoy its benefits if they desired (Genesis 2:16-17). The Tree of Life could keep them from death and be used to heal people. This tells us two things:

1) The tree's fruit would extend a person's life. It would keep them from growing older any further.
2) The human body could still be harmed, but if their bodies were harmed, then the leaves could be used to heal them.

When we understand the background of the Tree of Life, it is easy to see why God made it. People would live their lives, and God gave them the choice to stay on earth longer than our bodies could naturally survive. This way, we could serve Him on earth or, by choice, pass from this earth to be with the Father. This is not to say they couldn't be killed by falling off a mountain, but their age would not destroy their flesh. Most logically, they would have to eat it on a regular basis, or we would end up with the same problem as before.

Being in a perpetual waiting game of when we will mess up and die. While here, they could use the tree's leaves to heal their bodies through possible sickness and injuries. However, when all of mankind fell away from Him, no one was left without a sinful nature. For this reason, he took away this gift (the tree of life) from man.

The other tree, the Tree of Knowledge, would become sinful to man because of disobedience, killing them spiritually as sin always does. This tree is where most don't understand why God used it. The answer is found in the fact that everyone who has been created since the time of Adam will have to choose in their life to accept or reject God. God doesn't want a robotic creature to be with Him but a willing vessel. Like Josuha once said, God puts life and death before us to choose. And every individual must choose to serve God or reject Him. Holiness and goodness follow God, and everything contrary to God is evil. God continually states that He is looking for a people who will be His people, and for them, He will be their God. Even more than that, God wants a loving relationship between us and Him. However, love cannot be authentic without the option of rejection. We must love God with the free will that God gave us.

The Renewed Earth

There is another reason why God planted the tree, but it is much more profound yet said in a simple way. God makes sure in each of His creations, He gives an option to reject or accept Him. This will sound strange to many, but this world is not the first or the last world, and the Bible confirms this. To be renewed means that the base of a product is kept, and the bad parts are thrown away or fixed to return it back to a "like new" factory state. For our world, the base of the Earth's elements themselves are old, but all the living things on it are only about 7,000 years in the making. Some of these past worlds stayed true to God, others entirely fell away, such as our own, while others split into two societies, one holy and one worldly like the New Heaven and Earth will do. Let's look at the scriptures to back this up.

- **The first premise: God is a just judge.**

Righteousness and justice are the foundation of thy throne
- Psalms 89:14a (NKJV)

God gives every one of His creations the chance to know who He is. We understand that God will not send anyone to Hell unless they deservingly merit it.

- **The second premise: God is a creator.**

We are not the first or last world with created beings. In fact, we are not even in the previous cycle of life on this earth we dwell on now. Since this is so new to many people, I want to clarify it. God gives us evidence of a world before us and details about the world that will come after us. Also, the Bible still has two more cycles or tones of life to go through before it will be erased from the universe. We will investigate this in detail in later chapters with the 1,000-year reign and then again in the New Heaven and Earth chapter. For now, we will examine some basic biblical facts supporting the renewed Earth worldview. God re-created this earth in 7 days about 7,000 years ago. That is what we will call our world or the current earth.

God likes to have a "good" creation because of His very nature (A Creator). In the beginning, God saw all that he had made and called it "good." If the creation is corrupted beyond repair because of sin. Often, God will start over. Doing this restores the Good and removes the evil. This is not an evil outlook on life itself; this is not allowing evil and the torment that follows evil to continue when the viability of good can be restored. For instance, if God had started over with Moses, then Israel could have had a much better outcome today than it has for the last 3,000+ years. However, Moses begged God not to destroy the people. God listened to Moses and granted mercy to them. The nation as a whole has survived but has had a rollercoaster of an existence. The second and more obvious story is Noah and the flood. Looking at just the stories of Noah and Moses, we see God is ready to take the faithful and start over or wash everything away and start with a clean slate.

- **Moses -** *"The Lord spoke further to me, saying, 'I have seen this people, and indeed, it is a stubborn people. 'Let Me alone, that I may destroy them and blot out their name from under heaven; and I will make of you a nation mightier and greater than they,'" -Deuteronomy 9:13-14 (NKJV)*
- **Noah –** *And God said to Noah, "I have determined to make an end of all flesh, for the earth is filled with violence through them. Behold, I will destroy them with the earth. - Genesis 6:13 (ESV)*

Suppose this world is the only one to have ever existed for all of time. Think about what would happen to the universe if this one-man Noah was also unfaithful like the rest. Does God create the universe, and it didn't work out, so He destroyed it and walked away forever? That would go against His very nature to be the creator. For God to see a fallen world and say I will wipe it out and start over again is the only conclusion that makes sense. This is because it is in His nature to create and maintain it. Thankfully, Noah found favor with God, and he recreated it instead of erasing it.

I would liken it to having a garden in your backyard. You can plant the most beautiful garden, but then some weeds start to pop up. You can remove them over and over, but eventually, they overtake the whole garden. Making it impossible to grow anything "good." The only logical solution is to plow it over and start from scratch. There is a point of no return for God, and when it's reached, God will label us for destruction. He is very merciful and patient with us. Think about how long God gave Israel to repent and change their ways. He sent many prophets and guides to help them, but when they passed the point of no return, he gave them over to Babylon for destruction. A godly king even arose, King Jeremiah, but it was already too late. God took Jeremiah from this world so that he did not have to see the destruction that was about to come (2 Chronicles 34:28).

If God has already done it in the past, and we see that He will do it again in the future, what more evidence do we need, or could we find, to show us that this is God's way of doing things? Perhaps a straightforward passage that says just that will help?

Gen 2:4 - These are the generations of the heavens and of the earth when they were created, in the day that the LORD God made the earth and the heavens, (KJV)

This word, generations, means to be the descendant of another. This all implies that we are not the first but one of many. You may ask, "Why don't we know anything about the world before us?" The Bible answers that as well. After this world ends and then the next one begins, God says this.

Isaiah 65:17 (KJV) - "For behold, I create new heavens and a new earth, and the former things shall not be remembered or come into mind.

The old world, who they were, and what happened will be erased from history, just like all the things of this world and all the stories that have happened to us. Even during the flood, if it was not for Noah's faithfulness. We would have never known the things that happened in this world between Genesis 1:1 and Genesis 6:9. Over 1,600 years have passed between Adam and Noah, and most of history has been erased. This is just God's way of dealing with His creation, and we see it over and over. When people are faithful to God, the world will blossom. We see this in history, like with David's reign in the Old Testament and the age of the Church in the New. However, when the world rejects God and our hearts and minds turn to wickedness continually, we will have to deal with the judgment our actions bring about. The only thing that will remain of the past is the names of the faithful (Isaiah 66:22). Why? Because our focus is on God, If God destroys a world like He did in the flood, we don't need to look back at their wrongdoing to learn anything from them. We need to focus on God and live for Him in the now. We can take the small revelations God has given us through His word and learn from them. Other than that, we do not need to seek more information and, in so doing, repeat their evil ways.

How Does the Bible Begin?

Genesis 1:1; - *"In the beginning, God created the heavens and the earth."*

     This translation is accepted because of tradition but is not a good translation of Genesis 1:1. The original writings of this verse are written in construct form. This is a very complicated topic, but I'll try to reduce the complexity as much as possible.

The first word of the Bible is;

בְּרֵאשִׁית = bə·rê·šîṯ

     Depending on a few factors, this can be read in either the absolute or construct form. Nevertheless, only one can be right.

If the first word is in an absolute form, it would read.

"In the beginning God created"

If the first word is in the construct form, it would read something similar to.

"When God began to create"

     To see which form the text is written in, you need to look at the word paired with it and the context it is used in. There is a lot of evidence to suggest that this is written in construct form. This has a huge change in how we would read the opening passage of the bible. I understand not wanting to create confusion and chaos within the church body. However, not accepting the truth and changing to meet the truth when it is revealed is even a graver mistake. The different reading of Genesis 1:1 would change the whole view of what happened at creation. The traditional view ends with a complete thought.

"In the beginning, God created the heavens and the Earth."

     This is a timestamp of when God formed the world from nothing. However, since this is written in construct form, the first verse does not complete the passage, and it flows into verses 2 and

3. It also changes the time stamp of "The Beginning" into the action of "began to create." Therefore, a better translation would be.

"When God began creating the heavens and the earth. The earth was without form and void, and darkness was over the face of the deep. And the Spirit of God was hovering over the face of the waters. And God said, "Let there be light," and there was light.".

This means the first act of creation in the Bible is not the world itself but rather the light being created in the world that was plunged into darkness. This would be a look at a world that was destroyed and completely covered by water. The flooded earth would be much like what Noah had seen on his ark. All life is dead; however, what we see here is much worse than what Noah observed. There would be no stars in the galaxy and no sun or moon. Only the earth, which is void and fully covered by water. There is a passage to reference this as well. During Jeremiah's rebuke of the folly of Israel, the Lord stops and gives the account of the destruction of the previous earth, letting them know that He is willing to destroy everything if it comes down to it.

Jeremiah 4:22-28 (KJV) - For my people is foolish, they have not known me; they are sottish children, and they have none understanding: they are wise to do evil, but to do good they have no knowledge. I beheld the earth, and, lo, it was without form, and void; and the heavens, and they had no light. I beheld the mountains, and, lo, they trembled, and all the hills moved lightly. I beheld, and, lo, there was no man, and all the birds of the heavens were fled. I beheld, and, lo, the fruitful place was a wilderness, and all the cities thereof were broken down at the presence of the Lord, and by his fierce anger." For thus hath the Lord said, "The whole land shall be desolate; yet will I not make a full end. For this shall the earth mourn, and the heavens above be black; because I have spoken it, I have purposed it, and will not repent, neither will I turn back from it."

We see the earth as it is in Genesis 1:2, but only this time it gives us more details about life that was lost. And that the heavens existed but were also destroyed in the judgment of God. Many will think this is about Noah's flood, but the flood did not affect the sun, moon, and stars. Noah's story still includes these things, and they are not done away with. Also, this passage says, "There was no man," yet 4 men and 4 women were still on earth, dismantling this argument.

Archeological findings support this passage, which shows that some ancient structures are 12,000 years old or older but very rare. All living things we see today, including bones and fossils, are from our current earth, which dates back only 7,000 years or less. God emptied the old earth from all living things or remnants of them and started it anew.

The Galaxies

If we look at our universe with this biblical thought in our minds. We can investigate the reaches of space and see all the old Heavens and Earths from the past. Each galaxy has its own creation story and destruction. The remnants of what has been are still there for us to see in our universe today. All these galaxies existed long before our own. With nearly 2 trillion galaxies estimated in our universe. Each has its own timeline of thousands or perhaps hundreds of thousands of years. We can begin to see how ancient the galaxy is. Each galaxy was most likely the focal point of God's Kingdom of Heaven. Starting at some point in time, long ago, showing us just how unfathomably old the universe really is. However, since galaxies are created and placed in the universe, positioned by the Lord's will, new and old galaxies can be neighbors. Giving great confusion to those who don't begin with a biblical presupposition.

When we come to understand that we are not the first or the last world, and in each world, God gives free will to His creation, creating the choice to serve or reject Him. The logical solution is that He started this world like He has many times before, with a choice. However, since Adam and Eve sinned from the start, all of mankind fell because of it. We have been trying to restore our connection with God ever since. The Tree of Knowledge was not

God setting us up for failure but our own failure to follow God. Humanity fell quickly, and we only have ourselves to blame.

At the beginning of this chapter, I asked you to think of four questions. I hope you were able to pick up some thoughts on each of these.

- **Q) Why did God put the trees (plural) in the garden?**
- This was to present to Adam and Eve the choice of life and death, blessing and cursing. The same is presented to us as well. Adam and Eve chose death, curses, and life in opposition to God's will. The blessings and gifts God intended for them were taken from them.
- **Q) Why did God create the Earth?**
- God's very nature is to produce life. He is willing to be a personal God to us. He knows us intimately and wants us to know Him in the same way. He wants all people to come looking for Him, and when they accept Him, He will be their God, and we will be His people.
- **Q) How did God create the Earth?**
- God is not a one-and-done creator. He has been creating for an unfathomably long time and will continue to do so after our world is gone. Our goal is to live in the here and now and serve God with all our being—to run the race and to receive the prize (1 Corinthians 9:24). Our Earth is a renewed world, and God has a few more plans to accomplish with this world before it ends.
- **Q) What was before and after the Earth?**
- Today, we only see remnants of the worlds that were before us. Demons, angels, and the current Earth are from the generations of the previous Earths. God will one day destroy this world entirely and make all things new. He will give His new creation life, and they will strive to be with Him. He will dwell with them and set up His new city on Earth. As Christians, we have faith and hope through our Lord and Savior that we will be with Him when He accomplishes all these things.

Chapter 2

The Trinity

Why do we need to understand the Trinity when it is literally trying to understand the infinite with a finite mind? All in all, it is impossible to grasp it fully. Nonetheless, God wants us to begin understanding who He is. He has put enough information in His word for us to be able to get a clear understanding of Him here on Earth. Knowing more about God is as essential as serving Him because you can only love what you know about. The same is true with God; the more you know, the closer you can become. You can expand your love and relationship with Him. You can see this in practice through your spouse, friends, and family. You didn't indeed start loving them until you knew them. It's true as Christians, we are to love everyone, and faithful followers of Christ do put that into practice. However, saying that you love someone named Mike Greer in California is hard when I ask how you do that specifically. Loving Mike is to grow your relationship with him through emotion and action. Showing love applies to everyone, for that matter, whether it's your spouse or closest friends; before they were in your life, you could not show your love. Therefore, our words, though said in truth, are empty until we put them into action. You can have a passion for humanity but not the person.

God is the same way, but for Him, He knows the very hairs of our heads, the intents of our hearts, and every thought of our minds. God knows us infinitely better than we know ourselves. Therefore, His love for us can be infinite. On the other hand, our passion for our Lord depends upon the amount we know about Him. At the beginning of our walks, we need a Savior. We then accept Christ and love Him because He first loved us. If we can grow to the knowledge knowing the hairs on God's head or every thought he thinks, how much more can our love grow to match the love He has for us? I understand this is foolish talk, but I only mean to stress the point. We must dig deep into Christ and draw as close to God in knowledge as possible. So now, understanding the why, let's get into the what and how.

The Trinity is the Tri-God head, the knowledge that three forms of God make it possible for heavenly, spiritual, and physical life to coexist simultaneously and interact with each other.

•God the Father—He is in Heaven, seated in all His glory and honor. He rules the universe and everything in it and is worthy of all worship and honor.

•God the Son – Heaven's High Priest, a singular being, and God's mediator between the physical world and the creator of all things.

•God the Holy Spirit – God's omnipresence and power, ruler of the spiritual plane, deals mainly with the spiritual plane, who manifests in the physical in the form of the elements at times (fire, wind, water, etc.).

Why is there so much confusion about the Trinity? I believe it stems from Jesus being a man but claiming to be God. This fact may cause confusion and raise many questions, but it always has, even during Jesus' ministry. I will go through a few common questions before our study so that we can start on the right foot.

- Q: If Jesus was God, did He have all the powers of God?
- A: No, Jesus said that He emptied Himself before He came in the form of a man (Philippians 2:6-7, but Jesus was 100% man so that He could be a perfect example, sacrifice, and High priest to us (Hebrews 2:17). He lived as we live relying on the power of the Holy Spirit in all things. He was still God in authority and could call down legions of angels at a moment's notice. He was still given the honor and respect of being God. However, He had the exact same power as

you and me. Yes, he was still King of the universe, but in the humble body of a man in every way.

- Q: If God was human, was anyone running the rest of the world or the universe?
- A: Yes, God still reigned in the Earth through the Holy Spirit and the universe through the Father. The Father and the Holy Spirit were watching over Jesus and the world the whole time (Mark 1:11, Luke 3:22, John 12:28, Luke 22:42, Luke 23:46, Isaiah 42:1). Jesus' ministry as part of the Trinity is to be our mediator between God and us. The Son is always in one place at one time. While the Son was in the flesh, He still fulfilled His role in the trinity. His role is High Priest and Mediator. He performed these roles in a different way while here with us. When looking at the earthly life of Jesus, we see God taking on two forms, two different ministries, occupying 2 locations (Heaven and Earth). This is just our first example of a clear distinction between the diverse forms of God that will be understood as the Trinity.
- Q: Why does Jesus have to be God? Why not a glorified angel or something?
- A: Jesus clarified that He and the Father are one (John 10:30-33). The Jewish leaders understood it so clearly that they tried to kill Him for it on multiple occasions. The Trinity is so connected that Jesus says to see Him is the same as seeing the Father (John 14:8-9). Jesus tells us that He has always existed (John 8:58), and all things were made through Him (John Ch 1). The disciples declared Him as God and worshiped Him. Everywhere else in scripture, angels don't allow a man to worship them (John 20:28, Matthew 28:9, Matthew 14:33). Angles are created beings where God has always existed. Finally, but most importantly, God says so Himself (Hebrew Ch 1).

With a few major questions out of the way, let's look at why we even must have a Trinity. The simple answer is that God's fully glorified presence is too much to handle. If God the Father were to inhabit the same physical space as us, it would utterly destroy us (Rev 20:11). His tremendous power and might is too much for us or the Earth to be able to withstand. However, as always, God makes a way. He takes on two permanent forms that can work in the physical world without destroying it. An important note to add here is the fact that when God takes three forms. In so doing, it does not diminish His power. Infinite divided by three is still Infinite [$\infty \div 3 = \infty$]. However, the Son and Holy Spirit's eternal forms are different in heart, mind, and strength than the Father, but they are the same soul. The Bible tells us that what makes up a being is the heart, soul, mind, and strength, all of which God possesses, as pictured in this diagram.

	Father	Son	Holy Spirit	
Heart	Spirit	Spirit	Spirit	e.g. - John 14:23
Soul	The Soul of YHWH			e.g. - Leviticus 26:11
Mind	Spirit	Spirit	Spirit	e.g. - Isaiah 55:8-9
Strength	Spirit	Spirit	Spirit	e.g. - 1 Chronicles 29:11

- Heart: Emotional state, nature, and desires.
- Soul: The immaterial essence, animating principle, or cause of an individual life.
- Mind: Capacity of thought and ability of reason (that which thinks, imagines, remembers, wills, and senses).
- Strength: One's ability to accomplish tasks within or outside the body.

I am not in any way trying to limit God to these four areas. God is infinitely more complex than what we can conceive, and the Bible affirms there is so much more to His being. Just as one example, there are 7 Spirits of the Lord (Revelation 5:6, Revelation 4:5). Trying to focus on all the limited areas that we are aware of would still be too complex. Therefore, for ease of understanding, we are just focusing on these four areas Jesus taught us about. While Jesus was here, He was in every way made like us (Hebrews 2:17-18), and yet still God. focusing on these four areas that define a person will help us define how the Trinity worked while Jesus was in human form.

The Attributes of Being

We have already touched on the attribute of strength and that God the Father limited His other two forms so that they can deal with the physical without destroying it. God does this because He wants interaction and relationship with the physical world. The foremost being humanity, His creation that He made in His own image. In order to have this interaction, He established the existence of the Trinity within Himself. This limitation of the Son and Holy Spirit should not be taken lightly. Remember, the power of the Son and the Holy Spirit have the power to create all we see around us. The account found in Genesis chapter 1 shows us, in part, the power that resides in these parts of the trinitarian Godhead.

Jesus, in His glorified form, can speak and create the sun, moon, and stars (Genesis 1:14-18). He brings forth animals and plants. Together, the Son and Holy Spirit designed mankind in their own image and gave life to man. Not only that, but the world's most powerful and wicked spirits were cowards at the very mention of His name. The Son is given all authority and rules on high. The Holy Spirit can manipulate the very fabric of reality and change it to the way He sees fit. performing miracles, signs, and wonders. When I say that their forms are limited, I only mean that in comparison to the Father.

The Son and Holy Spirit are not weak or feeble in any sense. They are God just as much as the Father is God. Only their presence will not destroy us. When we look at this in reverse, think of just how unfathomable the Father's presence is. God has limited the portions of Himself for our benefit so we can know Him through other forms of Himself, which are the Son and Holy Spirit. Therefore, the attributes of the Son and the Holy Spirit in mind, heart, and strength will not be the same as those of the Father. Nevertheless, trying to say they are weak is a mistake. I want to go into some detail about the differences between the Trinity but keep in mind the awesome power of who the Son and Holy Spirit truly are.

We will first look at the mind. Jesus says He does not know the day or the hour he will be sent back to collect the saints (Matthew 24:33-36). Since it is dividing the Son from the Father, therefore breaking the Trinity in the sense of thought and knowledge (which indicates the section of the mind) and saying, "only the Father knows," then it should be safe to assume that the Holy Spirit doesn't know as well. Jesus is aware of the Trinity, and for Him to make the statement that only one of them knows this statement lets us know that the other two are limited, to an extent, in their minds and knowledge.

Another aspect is the will. The will is the combination of what the heart intends to do and what the mind goes forth to accomplish (Romans 10:10). The purpose of the Son is to be the High Priest to humanity for the Father (Hebrews 4:14). It is not the place of the Father to be the bridge between God and man, rather it is the Son's place. He is the one who makes sacrifices and brings gifts to God on behalf of society (Hebrew 5:1). He is the mediator between God and us. In comparison, the Holy Spirit's job is to work on and dwell within man's heart. He brings them to salvation and sanctification through His power. The will of each part has a task to accomplish outside of the Father. The Father is to be worshiped, to be the God to His people, and to receive those who have found salvation through His Son and Holy Spirit. What the Father does is far beyond our understanding, and it has not been fully revealed to us. We know our roles and what our part is. We are to be willing vessels that Jesus can present to the Father as holy, justified by the Son, and given as a prize to the Father in the end (1 Corinthians 15:24).

Let's look at the reasoning we have put forward so far. If there is a separation of mind, heart, and strength, why do we consider the Trinity one God? It is because they share the same soul. They are one being divided across the 3rd heaven, spiritual realm, and earth. If we could even begin to compare what this would be like for ourselves, what could we possibly compare it to? I think about it as if you made copies of yourself, but not in the way of making a clone independent of yourself. Instead, it is an extension of you that is a perfect and connected copy of you. Whenever one of these extensions does something, you would have done it. (This is a human thought concept, and it is not applied to God). If one of you were to marry, they would all be married. If one were to sin, they would all be guilty. If one were to have judgment passed on them, they would all suffer the consequences. Anything and everything about the soul of each individual is linked to the other copies of yourself. In the same way, God's soul is connected, but remember that God is a spirit, and His existence, overall, is different than our own.

When applying this same concept to the Holy Trinity, if Jesus forgives sin, then God forgave it; if one passes judgment, then they all passed that judgment at the exact moment in time. If one is worshipped, they are all honored. This is not to say that God has to forgive if Jesus forgives, but if Jesus forgives, God is forgiving as well because they are the same soul. Any spiritual actions are being done across space and time in one accord as one singular entity. This is an example of what the Church should be: Separate bodies (or rather parts of the body (1 Cor 12:12) but one body and one mission. Some may ask, does God have a soul? Yes (Leviticus 26:11; Judges 10:16, Zechariah 11:8). The most potent verse to show this is Isaiah 42:1

"Behold! My Servant whom I uphold, My Elect One in whom My Soul delights! I have put My Spirit upon Him; He will bring forth justice to the Gentiles." (NKJV)

God's soul delights in the Son, and the Holy Spirit works with the Son in all things. The Holy Spirit rested upon Jesus during His mission on earth, helping Him when in His human form—a great picture of the wills and missions put forth and acted out in the Trinity. The Godhead will never be against each other. Instead, He stays in the state of "being one," and everyone does the will of the Father. As we read, "for a house divided against itself will fall"; in this case, the universe itself would fall apart. In connection to John 10:30, "My Father and I are One," we can see it is the soul that makes the Trinity "one."

At one point in time, the eternal soul of the Father/Son/Holy Spirit was in the flesh, and we call Him Jesus. God's soul resided in the Son before and after His mission as the Christ. To understand how important a soul is, we have to understand that the soul is all you are. The only eternal and valuable part that defines who you are. It's not your mind, heart, or strength, only the soul. The connection of the soul of God within the Trinity is most clearly seen when we study the life of Jesus and how this applied when He spoke these words: "The Father and I are one." When Jesus had a heart of flesh, mind of flesh, and strength of flesh, He and the Father were one. Then, when Jesus died on the cross, and His body was laid in the tomb, His fleshly mind, fleshly heart, and all His physical fleshy strength were cold and dead. Even then, Jesus was still one with the Father, still alive (1 Peter 3:19) and still God. In the body, Jesus was God, and out of the body, Jesus was God. When He was out of the body, He was just a soul, yet He was still God.

Trinity at the time of Jesus' Ministry

	Father	Son	Holy Spirit
Heart	Spirit	Flesh	Spirit
Soul	The Soul of YHWH		
Mind	Spirit	Flesh	Spirit
Strength	Spirit	Flesh	Spirit

Trinity during the time of Jesus in the Tomb

	Father	Son	Holy Spirit
Heart	Spirit	N/A	Spirit
Soul	The Soul of YHWH		
Mind	Spirit	N/A	Spirit
Strength	Spirit	N/A	Spirit

The Importance of the Soul

The soul, in itself, is not a lump of mindless spiritual mass. Instead, it contains the whole of an individual, but only in an intangible form. Think about it like a car with or without an engine. Once an engine stops, the shell of the car, no matter how beautiful, is useless. Also, an engine outside of the shell of the car can run, but without an axle to turn, it can never move. Both a soul and a body must be presently integrated into one complete being in order to have permanent placement and impact on any plane of existence. One day, our engine (soul) will be taken out and placed in a better spiritual body that won't decay. God gives us a physical body on earth for our soul to inhabit so we can live an earthly physical life. Then, after we finish here on earth, we will receive a glorified spiritual body to live in, to do work and worship in the spiritual realm (1 Corinthians 15:53-55). The soul is like the wind trying to move a boulder; it's unable to do very much on its own, but just being a soul, we can think, talk, and move. We see this in the story of Lazarus and the Rich man (Luke 16:19-31). Also, when Saul calls on Samuel after death, the soul needs a spiritual body or physical body to live in either plane fully and be able to interact and work within it. Those who are not yet given their final form are called dead for a reason, and they are in a state of rest until the next stage of the world comes to be. They are not necessarily asleep or unconscious but are just waiting and watching until the next stage of the earth.

What is the thing that makes up you, the part of you that has its being?

"Before I formed thee in the belly I knew thee, and before thou camest forth out of the womb I sanctified thee, and I ordained thee a prophet unto the nations." - Jeremiah 1:5 (KJV)

"For thou didst form my inward parts: Thou didst cover me in my mother's womb. I will give thanks unto thee; for I am fearfully and wonderfully made: Wonderful are thy works; And that my soul knoweth right well. My frame was not hidden from thee, When I was made in secret, And curiously wrought in the lowest parts of the Earth. Thine eyes did see my unformed substance; And in thy book,

they were all written, Even the days that were ordained for me, When as yet there was none of them. How precious also are thy thoughts unto me, O God! How great is the sum of them! If I should count them, they are more in number than the sand: When I awake, I am still with thee." - Psalm 139:13-18 (ASV)

Before your body was fully formed, at the moment of conception, you had no brain to think, no lungs to breathe, and no heart to beat; still, you were you! When you were conceived, your soul was attached to your flesh, and in that way, you became a living image of God. God put together your living soul & the single cell of flesh with all the DNA code that began forming your body. We understand that, as humans, we are not created either physically or mentally like God. Rather, we are an image of God because we are a living soul inside of a body. God is a glorified body with a soul. We are a physical body with a soul. His body is eternal; ours is temporary. His soul is all-powerful; ours was created by His power when He breathed into Adam (Gen 2:7). Our souls are not on the same level as God but rather a finite image of His. At the end of this physical life, when we put off this earthly form, our mind, heart, and strength will all turn to dust, but our soul will depart, and you (your soul) will go to be with the Lord.

As a side note, this speaks loudly to the debate on abortion. To murder is to kill the image of God, to separate the human soul from the flesh, leaving behind an absence of life that was once present; doing this is murder. When does the person become a person? From the moment of conception, when the soul and flesh are knit together.

Difference Between God's Soul and Our Own?

Jesus & Holy Spirit are born of God; they are begotten of God. The Son in the physical plane of existence & Holy Spirit in the Spiritual. Whenever something bears a child, that thing is an image of the Father that bore them. A tree seed will be a tree, and a giraffe will be a giraffe. So, when a human gives birth to a child, that child is also a human. When God begets a Son, they are God because the thing that is foremost can only produce what it itself is.

Therefore, the Father is God, the Son is God, & the Holy Spirit is God, but there is only one God.

Isaiah 45:5a (ESV) - "I am the Lord, and there is no other; Besides Me, there is no God".

One God and only one, making them all one entity. When we see one part of the Trinity, we see at once all of whom God is. When we have the Holy Spirit residing in us, we have the Son and Father as well. We are not gods but rather the artistry God made with His beautiful hands. He breathed into us, making a living soul, and God loves us so much that He came and died so that we could have life and life more abundantly (John 10:10)

A Gamer's Example

Think about a video game, more specifically, an online RPG (role-play game). For it to work, you must have a designer who codes the game and watches over it. You must be able to make changes to the code and operating system. Next, you need a power source and main frame to run the code and keep everything in working order. Then, you can create all the different types of characters in the game. If the programmer wants to interact with others in the game, they will build a character inside the game to interact with all the free agents who are also plugged into the game. The creator of the game can use the avatar to interact with the other avatars in the game, even though none of it is done in the real world. The avatar is an image of the creator but not the creator Himself. God has done almost the same thing.

Though there are a lot of flaws in this example, it can get our brain turning in the right direction to understand. God lives in actual reality, not ours; this world (Earth) is only temporary. To determine where reality is, you must look at which is created and which is the creator, which parishes and which one is eternal. Where God dwells is the actual reality; we are now only living in his temporary creation. His Holy Spirit is the life code, power, and overseer that keeps His creation on track. Then His Son, who is God, can interact with us by taking on a form that is usable in this temporary existence. This imagery might help you understand the planes of existence that God's three forms inhabit. One must watch over all His creations, one must power and care for creation, and one must have a personal connection with the creation. Nevertheless, they are still only one entity working on different planes of existence. This is a thought process, and no perfect human example exists, but it might help some be able to visualize it.

The Planes of Existence

We know of at least three planes of existence: our physical plane, the spiritual plane in which angels and the Holy Spirit dwell, and the creational plane in which God the Father exists.

1. **The Physical Plane**—We are accustomed to thinking about things from our own physical plane, so there is not much to discuss. It is what we can see, touch, taste, etc. We live in this physical plane until we pass on from this life.

2. **The Spiritual Plane** - Overlaps our own. The Bible says that a spiritual realm is all around us, but we can't see them.

3. **The Creation Plane** – God's dwelling and the true reality of existence. Everything in the first two planes is created and maintained from this plane and is known better as the 3rd heaven

2 Kings 6:16-17 - So he answered, "Do not fear, for those who are with us are more than those who are with them." And Elisha prayed, and said, "LORD, I pray, open his eyes that he may see." Then the LORD opened the eyes of the young man, and he saw. And behold, the mountain was full of horses and chariots of fire all around Elisha.

Spiritual entities can inhabit the same space as us, but we can only interact with them when they want us to, giving us some logical insights. We should recognize two things: First, their plane of existence overlaps our own, and second, it is higher than ours.

This is Sam, and Sam has a box with a heart in it. Sam is a two-dimensional man living in a two-dimensional world. The heart is Sam's most desired treasure. Sam has inspected the box, which is closed on all sides, with no way for anyone to steal the heart. Unfortunately, Sam doesn't know about you. You are a three-dimensional person living in a three-dimensional world. Sam is only a small part of your world; if you want to, you can reach in and take Sam's heart out of the box. Sam would never be able to see you doing this or understand how someone broke into the box and got the heart out of it. This is a lot like how the spiritual world can affect us. It exists on a higher plane than our own and doesn't have to obey the rules of our world. We see this in how those with spiritual bodies can do things impossible for us. They can also do things to us that defy scientific reason. Such as taking someone from one place and dropping him into another (Acts 8:39-40), walking through walls (John 20:19), and closing the mouths of lions (Daniel 6:16–23). If we would sit and make a list of all the ways the spiritual plane has affected our physical plane in the Bible alone, it would be a very long list. These things seem impossible. However, it makes more sense when we understand a higher plane can always affect a lower reality in obscure ways that only seem impossible from the lower dimension's understanding. Much like how Sam can't understand how someone stole his heart, we also have difficulties understanding God's works in our world. On top of that, God, being the creator, can do or change things at will. Remember, He is the programmer, and if He changes the programming like making a donkey talk (Numbers 22:21-39), then He is free to do just that.

Hebrews 11:3 - By faith we understand that the worlds were framed by the word of God, so that the things which are seen were not made of things which are visible. (NKJV)

Although it's hard to imagine the spiritual plane as a fourth-dimensional plane that can impose impossible things onto our third-dimensional plane, we can still accept that it is a reality and that God continually works in this way. We do not need to understand it fully, but we can understand that it is real, that it is the reality above our own, and that God's reality has more power in every way. The Bible clearly shows the immense power wielded by beings of the spiritual plane.

2 Kings 19:35 - And it came to pass that night, that the angel of the LORD went out, and smote in the camp of the Assyrians an hundred fourscore and five thousand: and when they arose early in the morning, behold, they were all dead corpses. (KJV)

How can one angel go out and kill 185,000 soldiers in one night? Given the average length of a long night, say a 12-hour night, that would be over four people per second for twelve hours. There are also all the other accounts of things angels do through scriptures, especially in the book of Revelation. How can this be? It is because the spiritual plane is higher than ours in every way. The spiritual plane exists in a 4th dimension compared to our own. Suppose we consider the physical world as the 1st perceivable plane of existence. Then, the spiritual plane is the 2nd type of existence that we see in the Bible.

Then there is the 3rd type of existence, which, if logic follows, would exist on the 5th-dimensional plane, or as the Bible calls it, the 3rd heaven. Logically, God is higher than the angels or any other heavenly beings, so it follows that He exists on an even higher plane of existence than the heavenly host. The spiritual plane of the angels and the Holy Spirit share our first and 2nd heaven (Sky and Space). They are in time with us. However, the 3rd heaven is where God the Father dwells. This is also where Jesus is at the Father's right hand until the time of the rapture. A form of overlap is always happening between the 3rd heaven and the spiritual plane. This is God's Kingdom and the Kingdom of Heaven. We also see the overlap between the spiritual and physical planes.

We see this when spiritual beings walk and interact with man in our physical plane of existence (Genesis 18). It helps when thinking about this to picture the 4th-dimensional spiritual plane as the waypoint into the 3rd heaven; also, the 4th-dimensional spiritual plane is currently the location of the Kingdom of Heaven.

This is the easiest way for me to perceive how this works visually. The universe is ancient, and to think that God is moving the Kingdom of God from world to world does not make much sense. Instead, the Kingdom of God would be in a fixed position outside of space and time. We ourselves are fixed inside of space and time, and our existence within space and time contains our planet,

The universe on top of God's alter, in the 3rd heaven

galaxy, and entire universe. I believe a good visual would be an orb or cloud-type object resting on God's altar in the Father's throne room. The spiritual plane connects God's kingdom to all points throughout the universe itself. The Lord allows work to be done in the active location of our Universe and where He is seeking His people. Also, remember that the spiritual link between the 3rd Heaven and Earth is recognized in the Bible as the Kingdom of Heaven and/or spiritual realm. The spiritual realm would take up its physical space within our universe inside the cloud in what the scientific community would consider dark matter and energy, making up about 99% of our universe. The angels ascend and descend from the spiritual to the physical to do God's work (Genesis 28:12).

Our universe would rest on the altar of Heaven. Before the New Covenant, as people died, they were taken by angels to Abraham's bosom, which we will soon see revealed as the Alter of the Lord. While those condemned would wake up in hell, a place within the depths of our own world like a prison, to await judgment

(Luke 16:19-31). However, there is a Great gap between hell and Abraham's bosom. The spiritual plane is the stairway into the 3rd heaven, and the spiritual gap between the two would seem very short indeed. Short enough for the rich man to be capable of calling out to Father Abraham for help (Luke 16:24-25).

After the New Covenant was established and Jesus justified mankind, He changed everything about what happens at death. We no longer have separation away from God, and we could go and be with the Son after we die. Jesus established the Kingdom of Heaven; this Kingdom resides in our universe and in our timeline. This is where we go when we die as Christians (2 Corinthians 5:8). Jesus set up His new kingdom in the spiritual realm (Daniel 2) until the White Throne Judgment. In the end, Jesus will hand the Kingdom of Heaven over to the Father and begin it all over again.

All this setup and separation of realms is for our benefit. So that we can continue to exist physically and try to reach our goal, which is to enter the Kingdom of God and be with the Father. We are striving to spend eternity with the Father in the end. This is a complex topic, and it is even more complex than some would want to venture into. I am eagerly expecting to see it for myself, and I know so many others are as well.

God's Roll in the Planes of Existence

The placement of the Kingdom of God, the Kingdom of Heaven, and physical existence plays a role in the Godhead's physical attributes and roles within the Trinity. Each plane of existence requires an external body that will allow Him to work and rule over each one. For Jesus, His external body is mostly physical, even in glorified form, as we see in Revelation Ch 1, which is marvelous, for lack of a better word. The Son of God maintains a form that makes Him capable of working with us and enables us to interact with Him. When the Son interacted with Adam, Eve, Abraham, Jacob, Moses, Aaron, Isaiah, Gideon, Samuel, Daniel, Shadrach, Meshach, and Abednego, and at least 70 others, He was in a glorified form. Still, he maintained a physical presence on this earth. When we read stories of Moses asking to see God's glory, we

40

see He can pull away this physical form, which works as a mask protecting His creation from being overwhelmed to the point of death. Let's look at how each form of God works in the planes of existence they rule over.

- **Jesus, the Son of God** - Is God but exists in all three planes wherever He is needed. Our physical presence can interact with this safe form of God. His body can appear in physical flesh at any time (talking with Moses and Abraham). He is the high priest to mankind, our mediator to God the Father. He is the creator of all things. He brought our sun into existence with a word and dressed the Milky Way in its beauty. He "Emptied Himself" to live as a man and died to be our propitiation. While He was human, He retained His authority as God but became our example, showing that in all our weaknesses, we have no excuse not to live 100% for God in our lives. After death, He returned to His glory and is seated at the Father's right hand. Simultaneously, Jesus is also building a place for us to dwell with Him until the 1,000-year reign begins. Jesus has always been able to travel from God's throne room to earth to deal with His creation. He waits for the day to come and redeem His Bride. This is how the Bible explains His presence:

Revelation 1:13-17 (ESV) - and in the midst of the lampstands one like a son of man, clothed with a long robe and with a golden sash around his chest. The hairs of his head were white, like white wool, like snow. His eyes were like a flame of fire, his feet were like burnished bronze, refined in a furnace, and his voice was like the roar of many waters. In his right hand he held seven stars, from his mouth came a sharp two-edged sword, and his face was like the sun shining in full strength. When I saw him, I fell at his feet as though dead. But he laid his right hand on me, saying, "Fear not, I am the first and the last.

- **The Holy Spirit** – Is God; this form of God is omnipresent. He is in all places at once and on all planes of existence. It is the soul of God in an omnipresent body able to see and know all that is happening on all planes of existence. He was at work in creation, and we see Him in elemental forms

41

when He presents Himself to humanity. He appeared in forms such as whirlwinds, clouds, fire, water, and still small voices. We can come to God only through the Holy Spirit, and only through His drawing can we be saved. The power of God works in man to guide them to God. In the Old Testament, the Holy Spirit would come and help select individuals and leave them after His work was complete. The Holy Spirit worked in this way until Jesus' time when the Holy Spirit came and remained on the Son. Jesus has sent us the Holy Spirit (Comforter) to enter into those who find salvation and remain on us. Through His indwelling presence, we can do even greater works than Jesus did during His earthly ministry through the gifts of the Spirit. He is our guidepost in how to live morally and effectively for the Kingdom of Heaven.

- **The Father** – This is God's full form in all His splendor, majesty, power, and righteousness. He is the soul of God, but we do not know what kind of timeless or spaceless form He has. We can understand Jesus through His physical appearance and work. We have been given the most revelation about the Son, but realistically, we still know so little about Him. We can also grasp an understanding of the Holy Spirit; we can have an idea of the presence He takes on. However, of the Father, we cannot fathom the deeps of His form. No earthly presence or idea could help us begin to comprehend the Father. It is best to say His Glory is unfathomable to our minds. We only know what He is not; all the heavenly creatures and Spiritual beings in heaven that the Bible has revealed are powerful and unique. No matter how powerful any of them are, they are still too simple and weak to compare to who He is. The Father created them, and as the creator, He is more excellent in all things; the Father is far beyond all that has been created.

Chapter 3

Kingdom of God and the Kingdom of Heaven

In many ways, the Kingdoms of God and Heaven are one and the same and used interchangeably in scriptures, but they are also very different. Simply put, the Kingdom of Heaven is a part of the Kingdom of God. There is sometimes a distinction between where they are located and, most importantly, the timeline of the two. The Kingdom of Heaven started with Jesus's death and resurrection. He set up the kingdom with Himself as King, the Church as citizens, and the new covenant as the law. Then took a seat at the right hand of the Father. The Kingdom of God is different than the Kingdom of Heaven since it is an eternal Kingdom. It resides in the 3rd Heaven, which is outside space and time and is the final step for those who love and trust in God. The Kingdom of Heaven will, when all things are done, merge with the Kingdom of God before the new Heaven and Earth will be formed. God made this all clear when He gave Daniel the visions of the kingdoms to come. After the four earthly world-ruling kingdoms of Babylon,

Medo-Persia, Greek, and Roman were over, God established His kingdom, the Kingdom of Heaven.

Daniel 2:44-45 (ESV) – "And in the days of those kings the God of heaven will set up a kingdom that shall never be destroyed, nor shall the kingdom be left to another people. It shall break in pieces all these kingdoms and bring them to an end, and it shall stand forever, just as you saw that a stone was cut from a mountain by no human hand, and that it broke in pieces the iron, the bronze, the clay, the silver, and the gold. A great God has made known to the king what shall be after this. The dream is certain, and its interpretation sure."

Daniel 2:35b (ESV) - But the stone that struck the image became a great mountain and filled the whole earth.

All the imagery in this vision represents different kingdoms. The original mountain in the vision is the Kingdom of God, and the stone that was cut out without human intervention was Jesus, who set up His Kingdom of Heaven, which will grow to fill the whole earth.

The Kingdom of Heaven

The Kingdom of Heaven came from the Kingdom of God and will return to it in the end. This is strongly reaffirmed in the New Testament as God revealed more details. The timeline of the Kingdom of Heaven follows the Bride of Christ. When the new covenant started, Jesus began the search for His bride, which was fulfilled through the Church He established.

Luke 17:20-21 (KJV) - And when he was demanded of the Pharisees, when the kingdom of God should come, he answered them and said, The kingdom of God cometh not with observation: neither shall they say, Lo here! or, lo there! for, behold, the kingdom of God is within you.

The Kingdom of Heaven started after Christ's death and resurrection. The exact timeline is known because the Bible sets up not only its starting place but also its ending. For instance, John the Baptist was not included in its numbers.

Matthew 11:11 (ESV) - Truly, I say to you, among those born of women, there has arisen no one greater than John the Baptist. Yet the one who is least in the kingdom of heaven is greater than he.

Even though Jesus called John the greatest man to live, he was not enrolled in the Kingdom of Heaven. This is because the kingdom started after John the Baptist completed his earthly mission. Throughout the gospels, Jesus told us that the Kingdom of Heaven is coming soon.

Matthew 3:2 (KJV) - And saying, Repent ye: for the kingdom of heaven is at hand.

Matthew 16:28 (NKJV) - Assuredly, I say to you, there are some standing here who shall not taste death till they see the Son of Man coming in His kingdom."

Jesus told those who were standing there and heard these words that before they died, they would see the Kingdom of Heaven come. To define the timeline even more, the thief of the cross was not part of the kingdom. Rather, the thief was taken to Abraham's bosom, which Jesus called paradise. This is where Jesus and the former thief were after death, not in heaven but in paradise. Jesus then spent 3 days and 3 nights in the belly of the earth (Matthew 12:40). Then He arose and spoke to Mary and then went into Heaven. During this time, Jesus went away into Abraham Bosom after death (1 Peter 3:19) and then afterward went into Heaven after His resurrection, which was Jesus' time of receiving the kingdom. When His disciples asked Him about the timing of the Kingdom, he told this parable.

(A) *He said therefore, "A nobleman went into a far country to receive for himself a kingdom and then return. **(B)** Calling ten of his servants, he gave them ten minas, and said to them, 'Engage in business until I come.' - Luke 19:12-13 (ESV)*

After Jesus fulfilled His earthly ministry, the border of the kingdom of Heaven was opened. Once open, Jesus invited everyone into it. Jesus fulfilled the timeline of **(A)** in Luke 19:12-13 at His ascending to His Father (John 20:17). Now, we are living and doing the work mentioned in **(B)** of the same passage. Jesus referred to this access point into the Kingdom of Heaven as being open in John 10:1-18. Jesus called Himself the shepherd and the sheepgate at the same time, because we enter with Him as the shepherd and only through Him as the sheepgate. Once the passageway into the Kingdom of Heaven was opened, those who knew His voice followed Him into the Kingdom.

There were many reasons why Jesus came to Earth as one of us. One of these was to start His Kingdom and gather the citizens of Heaven into His Kingdom. Every kingdom or country must have subjects, and the Church is the citizens of the Kingdom of Heaven. Being a citizen of the kingdom means a great deal. You are a representative of the kingdom; when people see you, they get an idea of what the Kingdom of God and Heaven are like. Every person makes this same judgment call all the time. When we meet someone from Australia or Brazil, we begin to make assumptions about the foreign land that may or may not be accurate. There are a lot of people who don't like America just because the American citizens left a bad taste in the mouths of people from other countries they visited. As Christians, we are representatives of Christ and are here to be good stewards of what He has entrusted to us. First and foremost, we need to show the example of who Christ truly is.

For His name and the Kingdom, Christians have suffered relentless persecution around the world. However, Jesus has empowered His citizens by sending the Holy Spirit to be with us. Through the message of Jesus, walls spiritually and physically have been torn down. The message of God is growing strongest in societies where the heaviest persecution is upon the Church. Christ's message and the growth of the Church have smashed wicked world powers and brought salvation to countless people. This can only happen when His kingdom's citizens are good stewards and do not bury the gifts He has given them. Suppose we are fearful of what might happen in this life and bury our talents in the ground. Jesus will come and reject you as he did in Matthew 25:14-30. Being a citizen of the Kingdom of Heaven is not a day at a park filled with just rainbows and lollipops. It's an active call to duty where everyone has responsibilities and orders to follow. We are to enjoy the life God has given us and be ready for a call to action when our King calls on us to do something.

The Kingdom of Heaven and Rapture of the Church

The Kingdom of Heaven is active now, and we should be active as well. As citizens, our job is to gather as many as we can to follow after Christ. Then, and more importantly, we need to disciple others so they can have a firm foundation and not be swept away by the world. We are to be waiting and watching for the movement of the Lord. Then, one day, which no one knows, God will make a move and will begin the process of bringing the Kingdom of Heaven into full appearance here on the earth, where Jesus will sit on His glorious throne. The movement of God that begins this process is known to us as the rapture of the church. It will be the completion of Jesus gathering sheep into the sheepfold and the Bridegroom coming to collect His bride. The rapture is the wedding between Christ and His Church, and what a glorious day it will be.

1 Thessalonians 4:13-18 (ESV) - But we do not want you to be uninformed, brothers, about those who are asleep, that you may not grieve as others do who have no hope. For since we believe that Jesus died and rose again, even so, through Jesus, God will bring with him those who have fallen asleep. For this we declare to you by a word from the Lord, that we who are alive, who are left until the coming of the Lord, will not precede those who have fallen asleep. For the Lord himself will descend from heaven with a cry of command, with the voice of an archangel, and with the sound of the trumpet of God. And the dead in Christ will rise first. Then we who are alive, who are left, will be caught up together with them in the clouds to meet the Lord in the air, and so we will always be with the Lord. Therefore encourage one another with these words.

This is the same event as the ten virgins in Matthew 25:1-13 *(NKJV) - "Then the kingdom of heaven will be like ten virgins ....And the foolish said to the wise, 'Give us some of your oil, for our lamps are going out.' But the wise answered, saying, 'Since there will not be enough for us and for you, go rather to the dealers and buy for yourselves.' And while they were going to buy, the bridegroom came, and those who were ready went in with him to the marriage feast, and the door was shut. Afterward the other virgins came also, saying, 'Lord, lord, open to us.' But he answered, 'Truly, I say to you, I do not know you.' Watch therefore, for you know neither the day nor the hour.*

1 Corinthians 15:52-54 (NKJV) - in a moment, in the twinkling of an eye, at the last trumpet. For the trumpet will sound, and the dead will be raised incorruptible, and we shall be changed. For this corruptible must put on incorruption, and this mortal must put on immortality. So when this corruptible has put on incorruption, and this mortal has put on immortality, then shall be brought to pass the saying that is written: "Death is swallowed up in victory."

At this moment, the Church will enter forever into the arms of Christ, and the Kingdom of Heaven will be complete. We will be given immortal spiritual bodies ready for eternity. The Church exists in the time frame between Christ's rising from the grave and the rapture. After this, we will be in heaven with Jesus when He opens the seal, and the tribulation of the world begins (Revelation Ch 4-6). At the same time, the marriage supper of the Lamb begins. The Jewish marriage supper lasted seven days, and the tribulation and marriage supper will last seven years.

Revelations 19:9 (ESV) - And the angel said to me, "Write this: Blessed are those who are invited to the marriage supper of the Lamb." And he said to me, "These are the true words of God."

Many of those going through the tribulation will come to know Christ during the tribulation. Nevertheless, they will not be part of the marriage supper of the Lamb or given immortal bodies when they die. Their souls will remain under God's altar until the 1,000-year reign begins.

Revelation 6:9–11(KJV) - And when he had opened the fifth seal, I saw under the altar the souls of them that were slain for the word of God, and for the testimony which they held: And they cried with a loud voice, saying, How long, O Lord, holy and true, dost thou not judge and avenge our blood on them that dwell on the earth? And white robes were given unto every one of them; and it was said unto them, that they should rest yet for a little season, until their fellow servants also and their brethren, that should be killed as they were, should be fulfilled.

Revelation 20:4 (ESV) - Then I saw thrones, and seated on them were those to whom the authority to judge was committed. Also I saw the souls of those who had been beheaded for the testimony of Jesus and for the word of God, and those who had not worshiped the beast or its image and had not received its mark on their foreheads or their hands. They came to life and reigned with Christ for a thousand years.

For those who die during the tribulations, God will keep their souls under the altar until the start of the 1,000-year reign. At this time, they will come back in mortal flesh and live with Christ in the large new city of Jerusalem. They will not have glorified bodies but will have bodies of regular mortal men and women; they will multiply and live life on the face of the Earth. Those who live at this time will understand what a non-fallen world will be like with Christ as their King. Jesus will be residing on earth in the new temple. But at the end of this world, they will still have to stand before the White Throne and be judged for eternal life or death.

Those who are a part of the Bride of Christ and belong to the Kingdom of Heaven will be given rest, for our judgment is complete, and we will live with God forever with no worry of the second death. With this knowledge, please read this passage carefully.

Hebrews 4:1-11 (ESV) - Therefore, while the promise of entering his rest still stands, let us fear lest any of you should seem to have failed to reach it. For good news came to us just as to them, but the message they heard did not benefit them, because they were not united by faith with those who listened. For we who have believed enter that rest, as he has said, "As I swore in my wrath, 'They shall not enter my rest,'" although his works were finished from the foundation of the world. For he has somewhere spoken of the seventh day in this way: "And God rested on the seventh day from all his works." And again in this passage he said, "They shall not enter my rest." Since therefore it remains for some to enter it, and those who formerly received the good news failed to enter because of disobedience, again he appoints a certain day, "Today," saying through David so long afterward, in the words already quoted, "Today, if you hear his voice, do not harden your hearts."

For if Joshua had given them rest, God would not have spoken of another day later on. So then, there remains a Sabbath rest for the people of God, for whoever has entered God's rest has also rested from his works as God did from his. Let us therefore strive to enter that rest, so that no one may fall by the same sort of disobedience. For the word of God is living and active, sharper than any two-edged sword, piercing to the division of soul and of spirit, of joints and of marrow, and discerning the thoughts and intentions of the heart. And no creature is hidden from his sight, but all are naked and exposed to the eyes of him to whom we must give account.

Those who did not listen are both those left in the tribulation, being "those who failed to reach it," and those before the New Covenant. Joshua was following the law of Moses. Nonetheless, He could not bring them into the rest of the Lord because of a lack of faith, which is only found in Jesus, that is obtained in the New Covenant. We need to be constantly watching and prepared for His coming.

The Workings and Space of the Kingdom of Heaven

There are four parts to any kingdom:

- **King** - Is Jesus.
- **Subjects** - Are all those who have been saved through the New Covenant.
- **Laws** - Come from the Kingdom of God, which is eternally fixed by a morality designated by God's very nature. This means whatever is in God's nature to be good and true becomes good and true for us as well.
- **Territory** - Is in heaven and lives in the individual Christian for now. We are a piece of the Kingdom and have the kingdom's power resting within us.

Being a part of the Kingdom of Heaven is a lot like having citizenship similar to what the Apostle Paul experienced. Paul was God's elect on two counts because he was a Jew and an Apostle. Nonetheless, he was also a Roman citizen. No matter where Paul was, he was a Jew and a Roman. These were not just lines of heritage, but rights and power also came along with it. As Christians, we are citizens of the heavenly kingdom. The Holy Spirit has been given to us to guide us and give us rights and power to do God's will here on Earth. We are to continue the work that Christ started and be the light and power of the Kingdom of Heaven to our current generation until God takes us home.

There will come a time when the Kingdom of Heaven will be moved from the Spiritual plane to the physical Earth for 1,000+ years. This time will come at the end of the world's greatest tribulation. At that point the Kingdom of Heaven will remain on Earth for the remainder of the Earth's existence.

Isaiah 2:2 (NKJV) - Now it shall come to pass in the latter days that the mountain of the LORD's house Shall be established on the top of the mountains, And shall be exalted above the hills; And all nations shall flow to it.

Matthew 8:11 (KJV) - And I say unto you, that many shall come from the east and the west, and shall sit down with Abraham, and Isaac, and Jacob, in the kingdom of heaven.

Jesus's followers, including you and me, will see, feel, and experience the kingdom on earth firsthand as He reigns as King. Then, when the 1,000 reign is over, the devil will be released back into the world, wars will rage, and many other events will take place. Jesus will conquer all His enemies and, when all His enemies are subdued, will return the kingdom to the Father. This is the end of all things, and all those who find salvation in the Lord will be given to God as a prize. We will be with the Father and worship Him.

1 Corinthians 15:24–28 (ESV) - Then comes the end, when He delivers the kingdom to God the Father after destroying every rule and every authority and power. For he must reign until he has put all his enemies under his feet. The last enemy to be destroyed is death. For "God has put all things in subjection under his feet." But when it says, "all things are put in subjection," it is plain that He is excepted who put all things in subjection under Him. When all things are subjected to him, then the Son himself will also be subjected to him who put all things in subjection under him, that God may be all in all.

The Kingdom of God

The Kingdom of God is unlike the Kingdom of Heaven in that it is eternal. There is no beginning or end because the Kingdom of God is sourced by being the home of God the Father. Wherever the Father dwells, the Kingdom is in place, and the Father is the ruling entity. In comparison, the Kingdom of Heaven is a timed event in the timeline of this Earth. The Kingdom of Heaven comes from the Kingdom of God and will return to it, so it is a piece of the Kingdom of God. It is not wrong to say you belong to the Kingdom of God or the Kingdom of Heaven since we are bound to enter both eventually. To be in one is to be in both in many ways. The inhabitants of the world, namely Christians, will transition from this world into the Kingdom of Heaven and then later into the Kingdom of God when the end of this world comes after the Great White Throne Judgment.

Here is a more mind-bending thought: both Kingdoms' physical locations are separate in some instances and combined in others. As we said, the Kingdom of Heaven is now with the people; we move and operate in the Kingdom as its subjects. Jesus is in the Kingdom of Heaven preparing a place for us (John 14:3), but also sitting with God in the 3rd Heaven (Acts 7:55–56). The Kingdom of heaven is also in the spiritual plane, and we will be there for the marriage supper of the lamb. The Kingdom of Heaven is not fully in the 3rd heaven yet because it is given to the Father later and, until that time, resides in the spiritual plane inside of space and time.

3rd Heaven—5th Dimensional Plane
Kingdom of God—God the Father's Dwelling (Eternal)

And if I go and prepare a place for you, I will come again and will take you to myself, that where I am you may be also.
- John 14:3 (ESV)

Spiritual Plane—4th Dimensional Plane
Kingdom of Heaven—Home of the souls of past Christians
Place we celebrate marriage supper of the Lamb

Heaven and earth will pass away, but my words will not pass away. - Matthew 24:35 (ESV)

Physical World—3rd Dimensional Plane
Earth and the dwelling of man

Here we can see the crossover of how the 3rd heaven and the Spiritual plane meet. The 3rd heaven remains the dwelling place of the Father. The Son goes where He wants and is needed by the Father. The position of God's right hand is forever the sole ownership of the Son. Even when dwelling on Earth, the right-hand seat belongs to the Son. This term does not mean Jesus stays seated at all times, but His right to rule remains no matter where He is. When Jesus is dwelling in the temple for 1,000 years, His right-hand seat is still his position of power. Any earthly king does not need always to remain seated on his throne to be the king. Rather, they command the seat of power no matter where his physical location may be. This means Jesus can hold God's right-hand seat and simultaneously be in the spiritual plane with the Church. In these positions, the Son continually mediates on our behalf (1 Timothy 2:5) while also being with us in the Kingdom of Heaven (Philippians 1:23, John 14:3). Then, when Jesus ushers in the millennial reign, the Kingdom is physically separated from the spiritual plane. Jesus brings the kingdom to the physical plane on Earth. Splitting the mountain to make way for His city (Zechariah 14:4-11). During this time, the Kingdom of Heaven will continue on Earth until the very end of this world. Also, to be clear, the eternal Kingdom of God will remain in the 3rd Heaven as it always has.

What Does it all Mean?

What does this mean when we pass away today, or what if we are raptured for the Marriage Supper of the Lamb? Does it mean we enter the Kingdom of God or the Kingdom of Heaven? It's all a matter of God's timing when we should enter each. To be an heir of the Kingdom of Heaven means you are also an heir of the Kingdom of God.

Romans 8:17 (ASV) and if children, then heirs; heirs of God, and joint heirs with Christ; if so be that we suffer with him, that we may be also glorified with him.

Matthew 25:34 (NKJV) - Then the King will say to those on His right hand, 'Come, you blessed of My Father, inherit the kingdom prepared for you from the foundation of the world:

Jesus has been preparing the new Jerusalem for us to be heirs with Him and to worship, serve Him, and reign with Him (Revelation 20:6). This will all occur in the 1,000-year reign. It's important to know that, for us as heirs, our placement and location are not finished at death. We don't go to heaven to stand idly by for eternity. God has plans and things He wants us to do. Reigning with Christ is one of these steps when the 1,000-year reign begins. Defining the two means so much. When Christians die today, prior to the rapture, our souls will enter the Kingdom of Heaven and be where the Lord is.

2 Corinthians 5:8 (ASV) - we are of good courage, I say, and are willing rather to be absent from the body, and to be at home with the Lord.

However, we will not have our eternal forms yet, so we will still not be bodily prepared to reign with Christ for 1,000 years. Nor enter the Kingdom of God forever. Our souls are kind of in the state that those who died during the tribulation will be in. The difference is our souls will not be in Abraham's Bosom or under the alter. Our souls will be with Jesus in the Kingdom of Heaven. Like the souls that are in Abraham's Bosom, we will be awake and able to speak and learn and do things. Nevertheless, we will be just souls until the time of the rapture; we will be in a posture of waiting. Enjoying our time with Jesus in the Kingdom of Heaven. Our souls are held in heaven until the rapture. Then we return, the graves will open, and our souls will reunite with our physical forms and then be forever changed into a spiritual form ready for the next step the Lord has for us. We then will spend time in the marriage supper of the Lamb in Heaven. Return with Christ to serve in the 1,000-year reign, and after the Great White Throne Judgment, go into the Kingdom of God for the rest of eternity.

Conclusion

From the Kingdom of God flows all righteousness, morality, power, and honor. Everything begins and ends with our Father who is in Heaven. In Heaven, we see different beings that take every form imaginable. The 24 elders, the cherubim, the seraphim, angels, four living creatures, and others. Having this knowledge, it will make sense that they are all creatures either on their path to the Kingdom of God somewhere in their own timeline, or some of them are those who have already entered into the Kingdom of God's rest and serve God in the 3rd heaven. We don't have any history of them or what has happened before, nor do we need it. We can only wait to find out the rest of their stories when we see them face to face.

Chapter 4
The Old Testament

As of Right now, we are living in the Church age, but there have been many ages before and will be many after us. What I put forward here is only the History that the Bible lays out. There are obviously many other ages for which we don't have any information, but what God reveals to us is what He wants us to pay attention to.

- 1st Age – Adam and Eve in the Garden (short-lived)
- 2nd Age – The World After Sin (man on their own)
- 3rd Age – Post Flood (world reset/divided - God's choice of Israel)
- 4th Age – Moses and the Law
- 5th Age – Jesus's Fulfillment of the Law (Church)
- 6th Age – The Millennial Kingdom (world reset)
- 7th Age – New Heaven and Earth (world reset)

1st Age - Adam and Eve in the Garden

God has dealt with mankind differently in each age of our world. In the first age, we were meant to live in harmony with God, and God intended to dwell on the earth with Man. This was mostly covered in the first chapter of this book. Man had the opportunity to live with God, where God would teach Man His ways, He would be their God, and they would be His people. Man chose to be their own god by eating the fruit of the Tree. It's important to note who "god" is to you. The god in your life is the one who gets to decide what is right or wrong, good or evil. If you are arguing in your walk with the Lord about what He says is the good or the evil of this world. Then what you are trying to do is place yourself as the god of your own life. As Christians our walk with the Lord begins with a complete surrender that He chooses what is right and wrong. We are only to conform to the morality that God lays out.

Eve had a choice to make at this moment. She could conform to God's rules or try to be her own god. Eve could see the fruit would let her take on this role, and she chose to eat of it in defiance of what she knew to be God's ways (Genesis 3:6). She believed she could choose what was good and evil for herself. The thing she didn't know, because she didn't ask, was when someone becomes a god to themselves, they are in all aspects rejecting the true God, and His proper place in our lives. Trying to put themselves in an equal or higher place than the Lord. There can only be one person in your life who's in charge. If it is us as humans, we will fail and die. If we let God be the supreme authority, then we can live and live abundantly. Adam and Eve chose to take this role away from the true God, and because of that, they suffered spiritual death and obvious humiliation when the Lord drew near to them. When the one and only true God came into their presence, in an instant they came to the realization of who they truly were. Knowledge puffs up, deceives, and kills. It doesn't matter as mortal beings what we know, but only that God knows us

1 Corinthians 8:1-3 (ESV) - Now concerning food offered to idols: we know that "all of us possess knowledge." This "knowledge" puffs up, but love builds up. If anyone imagines that he knows something, he does not yet know as he ought to know. But if anyone loves God, he is known by God.

There is a strong connection between 1 Corinthians 8:1, *"Concerning food offered to idols,"* and what happened to Adam and Eve eating the fruit to become like God (Self-Idolization). Adam and Eve received the covering for their sins from the death of an innocent animal. Henceforth, they were forever cut off from being able to stay in the presence of the Lord. They were forced out of the dwelling place of God and were forced to do hard, manual labor to survive.

2nd Age - The World After Sin

After the fall of Man, God still dwells on the earth and dwells in the Garden of Eden but is separated from man. God can visit man, but man cannot visit God. Cherubim guarded the garden and would kill anyone who tried to enter God's dwelling place. The meaning behind the word "garden" is specifically a fenced garden. Sometimes, we get the picture of a jungle area, but it should rather be seen as a fenced city with one entrance to the east (Genesis 3:24). At the start of this age, the line of Cain continued to acknowledge God, but the descendants of Cain would soon rebel completely. Eventually, turning every heart of man against God, becoming evil with fleshly desires. Adam and Eve's third son continued to follow God, much like Able was doing before Cain killed him. However, those same people who followed and served God fell away from God due to sexual passions for ungodly women. Simply put, those who were faithful followers of God through the line of Seth began to intermarry with the family of Cain. Cains's family had become tyrants, doing abominable acts and wickedness. Their men grew in the power of the flesh instead of devotion to God.

Genesis 6:2,4 (ESV) - the sons of God saw that the daughters of mankind were beautiful, and they took any they chose as wives for themselves...... The Nephilim **[Bullies/Tyrants]** *were on the earth in those days, and also afterward, when the sons of God came in to the daughters of man and they bore children to them. These were the mighty men who were of old, the men of renown.*

As Cain's family line began to terrorize the world. The line of Seth took for themselves the beautiful women (who were most likely left as widows), mixing the two bloodlines. These children born to them had the prestige that came from the line of Seth mixed with the power of the tyrants from Cain's line. These children became heroes and great men in the eyes of the world. The world went from fear of evil men to a world idolizing the heroes that stopped them. Because of this, man fell into the pitfall of devotion to themselves, much like our present age. With Mankind worshipping themselves rather than God. It wasn't long before all the world turned fully into wickedness. This seems to be the trend when God looks at a world and deems it ready for judgment.

2 Timothy 3:1-9 (NKJV) - But know this, that in the last days perilous times will come: For men will be lovers of themselves, lovers of money, boasters, proud, blasphemers, disobedient to parents, unthankful, unholy, unloving, unforgiving, slanderers, without self-control, brutal, despisers of good, traitors, headstrong, haughty, lovers of pleasure rather than lovers of God, having a form of godliness but denying its power. And from such people turn away! For of this sort are those who creep into households and make captives of gullible women loaded down with sins, led away by various lusts, always learning and never able to come to the knowledge of the truth. Now as Jannes and Jambres resisted Moses, so do these also resist the truth: men of corrupt minds, disapproved concerning the faith; but they will progress no further, for their folly will be manifest to all, as theirs also was.

When the morality of the Church is lost because it mingles with the world, all righteousness will be lost, and only the wickedness of selfish passions will be left. The prestige of the Church becomes corrupt, and it uses the ways of the world to run or accept worldly doctrine. God strictly prohibits being unequally yoked to non-believers because intermingling will always end in destruction (2 Corinthians 6:14-16). The devil has tried to cover up this from our minds from stories of apocryphal books teaching angles having sex with women. However, by only staying within the true Word of God, you get the complete and true picture, showing us the lesson we must learn. We as mankind, are on a dangerous path of repeating this again. The Church loves to look good in the eyes of the world, to draw people into the church doors. This may seem like a good idea at first, but it ends with us conforming to the world and not the world conforming to God.

Maybe you're wondering who these heroes and tyrants were who stole the people's hearts from God. Plainly speaking, we are not allowed to know. This is just more confirmation of how God erases the history of the world's evil past. Even though it was within the timeframe of the Bible, we have minimal information and only a handful of people's names who lived through this age.

As the world pulled farther away from God, it fell into wickedness and chaos. God's heart was broken, and God gave the world a time limit of 120 years until He would leave the earth Himself and no longer dwell with man. When He does this, it will literally destroy the world by breaking up the foundations of the Earth.

Genesis 6:3 (KJV) - And the LORD said, My spirit shall not always strive with man, for that he also is flesh: yet his days shall be an hundred and twenty years.

This verse is often mistakenly thought to mean that man would be limited to only 120 years of life. However, Abraham, Isaac, and Jacob still lived well past this age, even over 1,000 years later, debunking this theory. Even Arron lived past this age 1,500 years later. When God created the human genome, it was perfect, and human's original design was to live close to 1,000 years. Through mutations in our DNA and a new environment of the post-flood world, humanity lived shorter and shorter lives until living to be 70 or, at most, 80 was a long life.

Psalms 90:10 (KJV) - The days of our years are threescore years and ten; and if by reason of strength they be fourscore years, yet is their strength labour and sorrow; for it is soon cut off, and we fly away.

The real meaning of this is seen not in direct wording but evident in the events that took place in the world. When it was time 120 years after the decree of destruction, God set into motion His plan, knowing that when He pulled His dwelling off the face of the earth, it would be an extinction-level event. The fountains of the deep would break, flooding the earth and simultaneously cleansing it of all evil.

Genesis 6:6-7 (ESV) - And the Lord regretted that he had made man on the earth, and it grieved him to his heart. So the Lord said, "I will blot out man whom I have created from the face of the land, man, and animals and creeping things and birds of the heavens, for I am sorry that I have made them."

This would be a reset for the earth, and perhaps God would have created a new Heaven and Earth or perhaps reformed this one. However, through all the wickedness, a man named Noah finds favor with God. So, God decided to restart the world with Noah, his sons, and their wives. As the ark was finished, God fulfilled His prophecy, pulling His dwelling (the Garden of Eden) from off the earth, and it broke the foundations of the earth apart, destroying everything with breath, saving only Noah and his family.

3rd Age - Post Flood

After the flood, the world began to repopulate, and once again, it would largely turn away from knowing God. We have the event of the Tower of Babel, and then the world was divided in language, culture, and land.

Genesis 10:25 (ESV) - To Eber were born two sons: the name of one was Peleg, for in his days the earth was divided, and his brother's name was Joktan.

Names in this culture carry meaning; you can often tell a lot about the person or history from the names given. When Jesus changed Simons' name to Peter, his life was never the same. This is not a defining source of information, but it gives us extra information to lean on:

- Shem – Breath
- Arphaxad - A healer; a releaser.
- Shelah – To send/ plant's offshoots or branches
- Eber - To pass over

Ebers sons
- Peleg - Time the earth was divided
- Joktan - Small dispute, contention, disgust.

- Reu - His friend, his shepherd.

The Bible aims to make a point with Eber's son Peleg, who tells us the world was divided, but before that, Eber's name was to pass over. So, it makes sense that if Eber passed over into other lands after the tower of Babel. Then afterward, God in an unknown event, separated the peoples by land in Peleg time. Dividing the seven separate continents apart into the ones we see today. The Bible has never been here to answer all our questions about history, and many events that happened are just lost in time. We can see the aftermath and make educated guesses, but we may never have a definitive answer. This event could have taken place in many ways. The two most obvious scenarios of events would be.

- God divided the Earth during the flood
- God divided the Earth later in Peleg's time in an unknown event

We don't have enough information to say which happened; we only know it happened at some point because of what we see today. If it was the latter, this significant event was summed up in this very short statement when Peleg's parents gave him his name. It does help answer many questions about how certain animals and people got to different parts of the world so quickly. But this does not mean God didn't use the flood to separate the world and guide the people and animals later. Either could have happened and still be logically sound; for me, the later breaking of the Earth is more reasonable.

After the division of mankind, the world began to be populated. There were many untold stories and prophets of God throughout the earth. We see this in the story of Balaam and Balak (Numbers 22-24). Balaam was a non-Jewish prophet used by God, who, though suffering many hindsight shortcomings, was gifted to be the mouthpiece of God. King Balak knew what power the true God had and that whatever God proclaimed through one of His prophets would come to pass. There were many stories of God proving Himself to the world that, like the earth separating, was lost through time.

Many people wonder how God will eternally judge the people of the 3rd age. Although there were mouthpieces from God, there was also no known moral law to live by. However, the Bible gives us a direct answer to this question.

Romans 5:13 (KJV)- for until the law sin was in the world; but sin is not imputed when there is no law.

If there was no set law, people could not sin in a way that would condemn them to hell. They did not have a law to teach them how to obey God. Therefore, they could not sin against God to deserve hell. Anyone who doesn't know the law when they die is not judged by the law. (Rom 2:12). For those who the law is revealed, the law becomes a double-edged sword. One side cuts down those who know it and refuse to obey. The other side opens the door to knowing God and having a relationship with Him and makes the way to eternal salvation instead of death.

Galatians 3:19-25 (NKJV) - What purpose then does the law serve? It was added because of transgressions, till the Seed should come to whom the promise was made; and it was appointed through angels by the hand of a mediator. Now a mediator does not mediate for one only, but God is one. Is the law then against the promises of God? Certainly not! For if there had been a law given which could have given life, truly righteousness would have been by the law. But the Scripture has confined all under sin, that the promise by faith in Jesus Christ might be given to those who believe. But before faith came, we were kept under guard by the law, kept for the faith which would afterward be revealed. Therefore the law was our tutor to bring us to Christ, that we might be justified by faith. But after faith has come, we are no longer under a tutor.

All throughout history, man has been in a waiting game. We often have a hard time seeing it, but we can have faith that God sees the whole picture and sets up a time that is best for each person at each age.

- In the 3rd age, they were waiting for the law.
- Those who had the law were waiting for salvation through faith.
- Those who have salvation through faith await the time we reign with Christ.
- Those who are in the reign of Christ will be looking forward to the time of the Great White Throne Judgement, which will bring them to their final eternal rest with the Father.

Since Adam, there has been a progression, and each group has been waiting for the next step. God has dealt and will deal differently with the people who live in each age. Not only in their worldly times but also in what happens to their souls after death.

The people of this age had neither grace nor the law. Therefore, God tells us that sin was not imputed to them. They were not guilty of breaking God's laws but also not made righteous and, thus, could not enter heaven. Furthermore, God divided Sheol (death) into two parts: one is hell, and the other is Paradise or Abraham's bosom. To be sent to hell, a place of eternal torment, you must sin in a particular way. You must disobey God's moral laws and judgments with the heart's intention to defy God Himself. Many have sinned since Adam and Eve, but without the moral law, do not know what they are doing; they could not sin in this way and, therefore, do not have those sins "imputed" onto them. There is a huge "but" to all this: if God did reveal Himself to them and then they defied the living God, they would be guilty of sin and sent to Hell. There were some before the law that could fall into this category; for them, they would go to hell or paradise but could not enter into heaven with God.

Luke 16:19-31 - .... And it came to pass, that the beggar died, and was carried by the angels into Abraham's bosom: the rich man also died, and was buried; And in hell he lifts up his eyes, being in torments, and seeth Abraham afar off, and Lazarus in his bosom. And he cried and said, Father Abraham, have mercy on me, and send Lazarus, that he may dip the tip of his finger in water, and cool my tongue; for I am tormented in this flame.........

For all of mankind, since the time of Adam and Eve, there were two separate places away from Heaven:

- **Hell** is a place for those who reject God and live sinful lives.
- **Paradise** is the holding place for those who can't enter Heaven nor deserve hell. This is not purgatory; purgatory is an unbiblical fable and should not be confused with these 2 biblical places.

These places have and will continue to exist all throughout mankind's history until the end of the 1,000-year reign.

And the sea gave up the dead which were in it; and death and hell delivered up the dead which were in them: and they were judged every man according to their works. And death and hell were cast into the lake of fire. This is the second death.. – Revelations 20:13-14 (KJV)

When Abraham and his descendants became God's chosen people, God placed him over "Death" (a place people go when they die, if not hell). This is the same place as Abraham's bosom, as seen in Luke 16. From that time on, Death was now called Abraham's bosom to the Hebrew People. The name has changed, but the places have remained the same throughout history and still exist today. The Bible never gives us any indication that they were done away with. Since they are still used and active in the 1,000-year reign, as seen in Revelations 20:13-14, all the evidence points to them still being used today. Especially since there are people in the world who still fall under the category of not having the chance to know or sin against the true God. The caveat to this is if God is revealed to you, then you must choose to accept or reject Him in this life. Leaving you Heaven or Hell as the only two options. You will only have one human lifetime when God is revealed to you; your choice must be made at that time. Some people who fall into this category and thus enter Abraham's bosom would be:

- Those who lived from Adam to Christ, who never heard the law or had the opportunity to serve God.
- Those who were faithful during the 4th Age under the law.
- Those today who are not able to make the choice to serve God, such as the mentally disabled or children under the age of accountability
- Those from the time of Christ who never get to make the choice because they have never heard the message of Jesus

This does not mean that no one went to hell to await the second death before the Mosaic law was established. Perhaps we even see some instances in the Bible of some knowing God's ways before Israel was created, therefore making them accountable. I am not the judge; only God knows. However, the evidence is that there were some forms of law and teachings of God before the

Mosaic law. One of these types might be Balaam. God had been revealed to him even though He was not of Israel nor had a written law. Showing God was moving in different ways in the world that we are not told about. If Balaam rejected God's words after knowing them and died in those transgressions, he would go to hell to await judgment.

We also see that the 3rd age was not without instruction on how to live for God. In the story of Job, he was a teacher of the people, and so were His friends who came to visit him.

Job 4:3-8 (NKJV) - Surely you have instructed many, And you have strengthened weak hands. Your words have upheld him who was stumbling, And you have strengthened the feeble knees; But now it comes upon you, and you are weary; It touches you, and you are troubled. Is not your reverence your confidence? And the integrity of your ways your hope? "Remember now, who ever perished being innocent? Or where were the upright ever cut off? Even as I have seen, Those who plow iniquity And sow trouble reap the same.

This was not a law we know about, but rather a leading through wisdom and revelations from God, such as at the end of the book of Job when God recorded His longest talk in the Bible. There was sin everywhere in the world, and thanks be to God for His mercy. Nonetheless, when anyone is given that chance to know about God and is presented with the choice to rebel against God's will and morality, then our "wage" for our sins is spiritual death and eternal separation from the Father. For Adam, it was one tree; for Israel, it was 613 commandments; for the Church, it is the rejection of Christ. God judges you according to what He sees fit.

God is a good Lord and King to those who are willing to listen and obey. If a person throughout any age of humanity seeks the Lord, then the Lord will work with them. That is why we see certain people find favor in the Lord throughout time. Even Abraham was born into this third age, and God chose Abraham to be the father of the next age.

4th Age - Moses and the Law

This is the age we see God choosing from mankind Abraham because of His faith. Then God gave him the promise to become a great nation known today as Israel, from whom Christ was to be born. With His chosen people, He passed down His moral law and established His covenant with them. During this time, the Son of God (Jesus) was called by another name, Melchizedek, the Prince of Peace. An important note is that each time God the Son sets up a new covenant with mankind, he changes His own name so that the change in the priesthood can be clearly seen (Hebrews 7:12). The Son of God has always been our high priest through all of History, but like when He changed Simon to Peter, there is a new chapter in life to be written. Therefore, the Son's role will change along with the name he will take for Himself. The first name we are made aware of was Melchizedek, then He took the name of Jesus and once again will change it after the rapture of the Church.

"'I am coming soon. Hold on to what you have, so that no one will take your crown. The one who is victorious I will make a pillar in the temple of my God. Never again will they leave it. I will write on them the name of my God and the name of the city of my God, the new Jerusalem, which is coming down out of heaven from my God; and I will also write on them my new name.'" - Revelation 3:11–12 (ESV)

This age of the Earth is the most significant part of the Bible, starting with Abraham in Genesis and ending with the start of the New Testament. There was no change in what happens at man's death. However, God re-establishes His connection with man through the tabernacle, the Ark of the Covenant, and God's mercy seat. His restored connection with mankind made a way to approach His throne for the first time since Adam. During this age, God sent his prophets to make the way of Christ's coming known to the world.

During this time, people still can't enter into heaven, but Abraham is put over paradise to welcome and care for those there and await the day for the resurrection of Israel. During the 4th age, the people to whom God was revealed had all the blessings and curses put before them. Their choice of following or not following after the Father decided not only their individual fate but the fate of Israel as a whole. With life and death before them, the wise chose life. Israel had many ups and downs. Some of their best and worst times came at this age. From such acts as King David's rule, Solomon's building of the temple, and the taking of the promised land. Then, we also see the lowest points: exile, slavery, and large-scale slaughter and death when they were disobedient. The prophets gave us the who, what, when, how, and why of the coming of Christ, and then there was silence for the last 400 years before His arrival.

Chapter 5
Christ and the Church

5th Age - Jesus' Fulfillment of the Law

This age was reined in by the virgin birth of Jesus Christ, the Son of God, who is our mediator to God the Father. The main point in the book of Hebrews is to define this change from the old covenant to the new covenant and the Son of God's position changing from the high priest of the old to the new and taking the name of Jesus Christ.

Hebrews 8:8-13 (ESV) - For he finds fault with them when he says: "Behold, the days are coming, declares the Lord, when I will establish a new covenant with the house of Israel and with the house of Judah, not like the covenant that I made with their fathers on the day when I took them by the hand to bring them out of the land of Egypt. For they did not continue in my covenant, and so I showed no concern for them, declares the Lord. For this is the covenant that I will make with the house of Israel after those days, declares the Lord: I will put my laws into their minds, and write them on their hearts, and I will be their God, and they shall be my people. And they shall not teach, each one his neighbor and each one his brother, saying, 'Know the Lord,' for they shall all know me, from the least of them to the greatest. For I will be merciful toward their iniquities, and I will remember their sins no more." In speaking of a new covenant, he makes the first one obsolete. And what is becoming obsolete and growing old is ready to vanish away.

Hebrews 7:11-17 (ESV) - Now if perfection had been attainable through the Levitical priesthood (for under it the people received the law), what further need would there have been for another priest to arise after the order of Melchizedek, rather than one named after the order of Aaron? For when there is a change in the priesthood, there is necessarily a change in the law as well. For the one of whom these things are spoken belonged to another tribe, from which no one has ever served at the altar. For it is evident that our Lord was descended from Judah, and in connection with that tribe Moses said nothing about priests. This becomes even more evident when another priest arises in the likeness of Melchizedek, who has become a priest, not on the basis of a legal requirement concerning bodily descent, but by the power of an indestructible life. For it is witnessed of him, "You are a priest forever, after the order of Melchizedek."

When Jesus stepped into the world, just about everything changed, and everything that remained was about to change as well. Jesus, who is one-third of the trinity, emptied Himself from His glorified spiritual body and His throne. The Son entered into human flesh as the Holy Spirit formed the new body inside of Mary and placed God's soul into the flesh, becoming the Christ.

Matthew 1:18 (NKJV) - Now the birth of Jesus Christ was as follows: After His mother Mary was betrothed to Joseph, before they came together, she was found with child of the Holy Spirit.

The Son was made a man in every way, with all our limitations and full reliance on the Holy Spirit. He was not all omnipotent, omnipresent, or omniscient. He lived just like you and me and even went without the Holy Spirit residing on Him until His baptism. This was to show that the Law of Moses can be fulfilled properly and with a heart burning for the Father. After His baptism, the Holy Spirit rested on Him for the remainder of His ministry (John 1:32-33). Jesus relied on the Holy Spirit for everything during His ministry and was our example of how to live in our current age. Through Jesus' example, we can know how to work in the power of the Holy Spirit and how to rely on the Holy Spirit's leadership.

Christ's life is far more like ours than most people think about. He lived as a baby and child and had to come to the age of accountability. Children before this age are incapable of sin because they are still without the understanding of right and wrong. After Jesus came to this age of accountability, anywhere between two to four years old, He chose to listen to the Father and obey. Many wonder what baby Jesus was like, and He was just like every other baby. He cried, ate, and pooped. He woke up at 2 & 3 am screaming and cried endlessly for His needs to be met. He had to be cleaned and fed the same way Mary and Joseph had to take care of their other children. Jesus was not pretending during those diaper changes. Rather, Jesus (God) had to learn how to be potty trained, just like you and me.

Isaiah 7:14 -15 (ESV) - Therefore the Lord himself will give you a sign. Behold, the virgin shall conceive and bear a son, and shall call his name Immanuel. He shall eat curds and honey when he knows how to refuse the evil and choose the good.

When He reached the age of accountability, He was honorable to His Father on earth and in heaven in all things. By 13, He was already capable of teaching others in the temple. He and His family had many struggles in life to deal with, even the loss of His earthly father, Joseph. Through all of it, He lived faithfully and sinlessly to give us a perfect example of how to live ourselves. Even in the face of life's greatest struggles, Jesus remained pure. Jesus had not yet changed the law of the old covenant and lived it out the way God originally intended it for all of Israel to do. Jesus prepared those closest to Him to bring up the Church (His bride) after He left. At the end of His ministry, He became the sacrificial Lamb of atonement for the whole world. This was to fulfill the whole law as laid out in Leviticus 16. Jesus did not have to do the sacrifice of the bull because He had no sin. Jesus stood in place of both the sacrificial and the living scapegoat, as well as the High Priest.

Leviticus 16:7-22 (ESV) - Then he shall take the two goats and set them before the Lord at the entrance of the tent of meeting. And Aaron shall cast lots over the two goats, one lot for the Lord and the other lot for Azazel. And Aaron shall present the goat on which the lot fell for the Lord and use it as a sin offering, but the goat on which the lot fell for scapegoat shall be presented alive before the Lord to make atonement over it, that it may be sent away into the wilderness to scapegoat...... "Then he shall kill the goat of the sin offering that is for the people and bring its blood inside the veil and do with its blood .... sprinkling it over the mercy seat and in front of the mercy seat. Thus he shall make atonement for the Holy Place, because of the uncleannesses of the people of Israel and because of their transgressions, all their sins. And so he shall do for the tent of meeting, which dwells with them in the midst of their uncleannesses. No one may be in the tent of meeting from the time he enters to make atonement in the Holy Place until he comes out and has made atonement for himself and for his house and for all the assembly of Israel. .... "And when he has made an end of atoning for the Holy Place and the tent of meeting and the altar, he shall present the live goat. And Aaron shall lay both his hands on the head of the live goat, and confess over it all the iniquities of the people of Israel, and all their transgressions, all their sins. And he shall put them on the head of the goat and send it away into the wilderness by the hand of a man who is in readiness. The goat shall bear all their iniquities on itself to a remote area, and he shall let the goat go free in the wilderness.

Jesus was killed and raised from the dead and lives forever. He can take on both roles of the sacrificial goat and the scapegoat. When we sin, two things happen to us spiritually. First, we are cut off from the Father because of sin, and because we are cut off, we can't approach the throne to confess and receive salvation. Second, our sin earns us the wages of death, which is the second death of hell. The first part is the separation of us and God. This happened with Adam and is passed down to all mankind who have lived. No matter how good we live, no one has ever earned our way into Heaven because the separation of God and man remains. The second part is once we willfully sin against God through disobedience, we experience spiritual death.

Jesus' goal was to repair us to a spiritual state where we were able to approach the Father and confess our sins to receive forgiveness. For that to happen, an innocent, living, breathing creature must die; the blood must be consecrated and given to restore us to a place where we are able to receive forgiveness for our sins. Their innocence stands in the place of our wickedness. Nonetheless, this part does not take away our sins; it only puts us in a position to be forgiven of our sins. For the old covenant, this sacrifice happened. After the blood sacrifice, confessions could be made, and then forgiveness could take place. However, the animal's blood was limited to that one time; if you fall back into sin, then there is no more blood covering you to bring you into the presence of God to ask for forgiveness. Therefore, the blood of a new sacrifice needed to be repeated repeatedly. Each time an individual sinned, a new sacrifice would need to be made to atone for it. For Israel as a whole, the blood was placed on the ark of the covenant. Here, it would remain for the year, and God accepted this sacrifice as a blood covering for the nation of Israel throughout the year. In this way, Israel remained God's blessed and anointed people. During the times Israel fell away from God's decrees, and there was no more repentance. His spirit left them completely, along with their protection. The blood on the ark for God's people allowed them to fulfill the law before God and bring their sacrifices individually to ask for their individual forgiveness of their sins.

Jesus' sacrifice fulfilled these requirements and established the new covenant. He became the eternal propitiation for that sacrifice. Jesus died on the cross, and His blood of innocence stands in the place of the animal sacrifice required. To complete and fulfill the law, He then resurrected and ascended into heaven to complete the law as a high priest. To do so, Jesus would need to put His own blood on the Ark of the Covenant (not the earthly one but the Heavenly Ark).

Leviticus 22:1-3 (NKJV) - Then the Lord spoke to Moses, saying, "Speak to Aaron and his sons, that they separate themselves from the holy things of the children of Israel, and that they do not profane My holy name by what they dedicate to Me: I am the Lord. Say to them: 'Whoever of all your descendants throughout your generations, who goes near the holy things which the children of Israel dedicate to the Lord, while he has uncleanness upon him, that person shall be cut off from My presence: I am the Lord.

Arron's requirement to be alone in the temple during this time was the same reason Mary was told not to touch Jesus in the garden (John 20:17). Jesus was still in the process of fulfilling the law of the high priest and had not ascended into heaven to present

His blood on the Ark of the Covenant. If Mary had touched Jesus as the sacrifice, she would have been cut off from the Lord's presence. After leaving Mary, Jesus went into heaven and placed His blood on the ark of the covenant in Heaven before the Father (Leviticus 16:7-22).

Revelation 11:19 (NKJV) - Then God's temple in heaven was opened, and the ark of his covenant was seen within his temple. There were flashes of lightning, rumblings, peals of thunder, an earthquake, and heavy hail.

Jesus would have placed His own blood on this Heavenly ark and fulfilled the first part of the law that required a blood sacrifice. Mankind is now restored to a place of nonseparation (Hebrews 9:24). After this establishment of blood, the next part of the ceremony can take place. The scapegoat is the part where the sins are removed from the individual. It is not until the confession of the sins that our sins are taken away.

Romans 10:9-10 (ESV) - because, if you confess with your mouth that Jesus is Lord and believe in your heart that God raised him from the dead, you will be saved. For with the heart one believes and is justified, and with the mouth one confesses and is saved.

1 John 1:9 (KJV) - If we confess our sins, he is faithful and just to forgive us our sins and to cleanse us from all unrighteousness.

This is not to say that you need to recite every sin you have ever made to have them forgiven. That is not what Aaron did or what we must do, but we need to claim Jesus as our Savior, recognize we have sinned, and ask for the forgiveness through Grace that Jesus is granting us. We can confess individual sins and should. It helps to talk with God about how He can help us not fall into these particular things again in the future. Nonetheless, if we ask God to forgive us and our evil ways as a whole, He will do the work in our lives. We see this in Jesus' parable.

Luke 18:13 (KJV) - And the publican, standing afar off, would not lift up so much as his eyes unto heaven, but smote upon his breast, saying, God be merciful to me a sinner.... went home justified before God...

Backsliding

Whenever we sin, even as Christians, we are covered under the blood to be able to re-approach the throne and ask for forgiveness. If we don't confess our sins and don't turn from our sinful ways, we will fall away from God and shrink back into the world. Hebrews chapter 10 shows us both the forgiveness of the repentant sinner and the backslider who falls away.

Hebrew 10:1-18 (ASV) - For the law having a shadow of the good things to come, not the very image of the things, can never with the same sacrifices year by year, which they offer continually, make perfect them that draw nigh. Else would they not have ceased to be offered? because the worshippers, having been once cleansed, would have had no more consciousness of sins. But in those sacrifices there is a remembrance made of sins year by year. For it is impossible that the blood of bulls and goats should take away sins. Wherefore when he cometh into the world, he saith, Sacrifice and offering thou wouldest not, But a body didst thou prepare for me; ..... I am come to do thy will. He taketh away the first, that he may establish the second. By which will we have been sanctified through the offering of the body of Jesus Christ once for all....when he had offered one sacrifice for sins for ever, sat down on the right hand of God; henceforth expecting till his enemies be made the footstool of his feet. For by one offering he hath perfected for ever them that are sanctified. And the Holy Spirit also beareth witness to us; for after he hath said, This is the covenant that I will make with them after those days, saith the Lord: I will put my laws on their heart, And upon their mind also will I write them; then saith he, And their sins and their iniquities will I remember no more. Now where remission of these is, there is no more offering for sin.

We are human, and even though His will for us is to go and sin no more, sanctified and to be perfect as He is perfect (Matthew 5:48). Oftentimes, our flesh gets the better of us, and we fail. If we sin again, we will once again be entrapped in death and found guilty, with our wages being the 2nd death. This is because even though we are forever in a state of the presence of the Lord, which allows us to approach the throne, confessing our sins and asking to be forgiven is still required. When we sin, that is us shrinking back, or what we would call backsliding. If we find ourselves at this point, we need to humble ourselves into repentance and turn from our wicked ways. Repeatedly, God is willing to forgive us; However, God does not want this type of life for anyone. He wants us to turn from our sin and reject all unrighteousness from our lives, and live wholly for Him. Nonetheless, getting lost in the world and dying in our sins is possible.

Hebrews 10:26-39 (ESV) - For if we go on sinning deliberately after receiving the knowledge of the truth, there no longer remains a sacrifice for sins, but a fearful expectation of judgment, and a fury of fire that will consume the adversaries. ..... It is a fearful thing to fall into the hands of the living God. But recall the former days when, after you were enlightened, you endured a hard struggle with sufferings.... But we are not of those who shrink back and are destroyed, but of those who have faith and preserve their souls.

We might mess up in this life, yet our goal is to *"Be holy, for I am Holy" (1 Peter 1:16).* God doesn't want any sin in our lives. However, if we sin, we will once again be entrapped with death. If we find ourselves here, we can again come to the Father, and He is gracious and merciful to forgive our sins because He is the living sacrifice and current scapegoat of the law.

Come now, and let us reason together, saith the Lord: though your sins be as scarlet, they shall be as white as snow; though they be red like crimson, they shall be as wool. - Isaiah 1:18 (KJV)

Unforgivable

Many people ask questions about what sins are unforgivable. We look at our lives and ask ourselves if God can really take away the wrong we have done. We have a hard time forgiving ourselves, so how can God forgive us? There is only one unforgivable sin the Bible talks about, which is the blasphemy of the Holy Spirit. If you have not committed this one sin, grace and forgiveness are awaiting you. Murder, rape, and little white lies can all be forgiven; there may be natural consequences attached to these, but the eternal accountability of these can be washed away. Nevertheless, there is something so grievous that will have such an effect on us that it stops us from ever receiving forgiveness again.

The next question should be, how do I know if I have committed this sin, and what happens if I do? There are two steps you must take in order to commit the blasphemy of the Holy Spirit.

1) You must know the Holy Spirit and be working in the gifts of the Spirit, doing the work of God's Kingdom

2) After you have experienced God in this way and choose to fall away into apostasy (this is not just sinning but walking away from God), reject His presence and existence, or speak evil of Him, then you will fall away forever (Mark 3:29).

Hebrews 6:4-6 (ASV) - For as touching those who were once enlightened and tasted of the heavenly gift, and were made partakers of the Holy Spirit, and tasted the good word of God, and the powers of the age to come, and then fell away, it is impossible to renew them again unto repentance; seeing they crucify to themselves the Son of God afresh, and put him to an open shame.

Q) Why can't the blasphemer receive forgiveness for their sins?

Since the Holy Spirit is our seal (Ephesians 1:13), and if we blaspheme Him, then God's seal upon us is broken and the blood covering keeping us in the presence of God is taken away. Remember, there are two steps to forgiveness. Once you are removed from the presence, no matter how much they call out to God, from that point on, they will forever be unable to receive forgiveness. It's like they are trying to do the portion of the scapegoat (confession) without the blood of restoration. As Hebrews 6:4-6 stated, they would need to have a new blood sacrifice placed on the mercy seat (Ark of the Covenant) again, which will not happen. That person becomes accursed and will never be able to approach the throne of God to confess and ask for forgiveness anymore. Sin will remain on them, and in the end, they will be cast into hell. Be watchful, obedient, and respectful to the Holy Spirit, trusting in Him.

You will hear many people say that once you commit the sin of blasphemy of the Holy Spirit, you will no longer feel the need for forgiveness. You will no longer feel the pull of the Holy Spirit for you to get right or close to God. This has some truth to it, the Holy Spirit will not pull on your heart anymore. However, Man can still have the same desire to seek God as they did all through the Old Testament. Unfortunately, they will seek but never find Him (Jerimiah 18:10-17). I believe the concept of no longer desiring God comes from the Apologetic argument C.S. Lewis proposed that every intrinsic and natural desire or need in our life can be met with a solution. If you are hungry, there is food; thirsty, there's water; and for humanity, there has always been a desire for a God or an afterlife. Since there's nothing on Earth that can satisfy this desire, then logically, there must be something outside this world to fulfill it. This is a great apologetics tool, but we can't unwrite biblical teaching for philosophical argumentation if the Bible states the truth itself and is contrary to the statement.

The Bible, in fact, tells us that those who sin in this way may still desire earnestly what they had before. Nevertheless, they can never have it, and a permanent mental shift will happen inside the person that can never be undone.

Hebrews 12:15-17 (KJV) - Looking diligently lest any man fail of the grace of God; lest any root of bitterness springing up trouble you, and thereby many be defiled; Lest there be any fornicator, or profane person, as Esau, who for one morsel of meat sold his birthright. For ye know how that afterward, when he would have inherited the blessing, he was rejected: for he found no place of repentance, though he sought it carefully with tears.

The exegesis of Hebrews 12 calls Christians to stand firm in the faith, take correction with humility, and learn from it. It says Christians should strengthen themselves so they don't "fail." Then, it likens Christians who blaspheme God by profaning the promise given to them to Esau Abraham's firstborn son. Esau's birthright was to be the inheritor of God's promise, just as we are the inheritor of the Holy Spirit. If you read Hebrews 6:4-6 and think about Esau, but the promise being his birthright, the connection that Hebrews 12 is making is evident. Christians can give up the promise of the Holy Spirit or count it as nothing, just as Esau sold it for some food. Here we see that Esau wanted the promise back and wept over it, but no forgiveness was attainable. There is only one unforgivable sin.

Matthew 12:31-32 (KJV) - Wherefore I say unto you, All manner of sin and blasphemy shall be forgiven unto men: but the blasphemy against the Holy Ghost shall not be forgiven unto men. And whosoever speaketh a word against the Son of man, it shall be forgiven him: but whosoever speaketh against the Holy Ghost, it shall not be forgiven him, neither in this world, neither in the world to come.

Even in the next world, this sin is so grievous that it will be one of the ways people will fall out of grace with God and be eternally damned. There are still more reasons that Hebrews is connecting this to Esau; it shows the change in the mindset of the lost person. God hated Esau because he fell out of God's covenant forever. Esau's mind changed into pure rage and hatred for the one that remained in the covenant (Genesis Ch 27 – 28). Esau planned to kill his brother and did what was dishonorable to his Father. He no longer cared about being the beloved son but lived for himself. When we see him later, during Jacob's return, he had acquired many worldly possessions outside of God's blessings. Esau's descendants turned to pagan gods, and throughout History, Esau (Edom) was subjected to Israel to serve it. Esau was never the same, but it was only one of the examples we have.

Judas was another who lived out Hebrews 6:4-6 exactly; he also had the mindset of loving Christ, which changed over to working against Him. Then, when he looked at his actions and could not bear the thoughts in his mind, he committed suicide. Judas was once filled with the Holy Spirit and could do mighty works in the name of God. Yet His falling away sealed his fate and corrupted his mind into self-destruction.

Three more examples are Hymenaeus, Alexander, and Philetus. All three were Christian brothers who became blasphemers after being swept up in false doctrine. Paul used them in his letters to Timothy as examples of people who shipwrecked their faith. Once again, we see them all become enemies of God's work and truth.

1 Timothy 1:19-20 (ESV) - holding faith and a good conscience. By rejecting this, some have made shipwreck of their faith, among whom are Hymenaeus and Alexander, whom I have handed over to Satan that they may learn not to blaspheme.

2 Timothy 2:15-18 (ESV) - Do your best to present yourself to God as one approved, a worker who has no need to be ashamed, rightly handling the word of truth. But avoid irreverent babble, for it will lead people into more and more ungodliness, and their talk will spread like gangrene. Among them are Hymenaeus and Philetus, who have swerved from the truth, saying that the resurrection has already happened. They are upsetting the faith of some.

2 Timothy 4:14-15 (ESV) - Alexander the coppersmith did me great harm; the Lord will repay him according to his deeds. Beware of him yourself, for he strongly opposed our message.

Paul was accustomed to the opposition in his ministry and even underwent many physical attacks upon his body for the Lord. However, these three men were different. They were brothers who became enemies. Timothy would have recognized these names and understood Paul's warnings. They became mouthpieces of the devil, spreading false doctrine that would cause many to backslide as they did. In today's Church, there is a significant issue: many people are compromising the Bible into lies to create social following groups. Precisely as Paul stated, *"irreverent babble leads to ungodliness."* In Romans chapter 1, Paul listed many sins that many shipwrecked churches have come to accept and preach today as God's ways.

Romans 1:21-32 (KJV) - Because that, when they knew God, they glorified him not as God, neither were thankful; but became vain in their imaginations, and their foolish heart was darkened. Professing themselves to be wise, they became fools, And changed the glory of the uncorruptible God into an image made like to corruptible man, and to birds, and fourfooted beasts, and creeping things. Wherefore God also gave them up to uncleanness through the lusts of their own hearts, to dishonour their own bodies between themselves: Who changed the truth of God into a lie, and worshipped and served the creature more than the Creator, who is blessed for ever. Amen. For this cause God gave *them up unto vile affections: for **even their women did change the natural use into that which is against nature: And likewise also the men, leaving the natural use of the woman, burned in their lust one toward another; men with men** working that which is unseemly, and receiving in themselves that recompence of their error which was meet. And even as they did not like to retain God in their knowledge, God gave them over to a reprobate mind, to do those things which are not convenient; Being filled with all unrighteousness, **fornication, wickedness, covetousness, maliciousness; full of envy, murder, debate, deceit, malignity; whisperers, Backbiters, haters of God, despiteful, proud, boasters, inventors of evil things, disobedient to parents, Without understanding, covenant breakers, without natural affection, implacable, unmerciful:** Who knowing the judgment of God, that they which commit such things are worthy of death, not only do the same, but have pleasure in them that do them.*

When we take all these things into account, it becomes clear why the Church is becoming such a battleground. Those who have come to the point of blaspheming the Holy Spirit of God have their minds changed to become enemies of the truth. Their love turns to hatred for those who continue to uphold the promise given to us by our Lord. The LGBT, abortion, and all the other evil movements in the world are not just planning to go to hell for their beliefs but to drag as many with them as they possibly can. Those who "condone" or have "pleasure" in those who do these things will suffer the same fate as those who commit the acts themselves.

It's important to note that not everyone who supports these godless causes is condemned to be forever lost. They can still find forgiveness and turn from their ways. However, those who have fulfilled *Hebrews 6:4-6* and then fail away into these things are lost, and these people should be avoided at all costs and cast out of the body of Christ.

Special Forgiveness

Think about when Jesus forgave sin while he was here on earth. There were times when people didn't even ask for forgiveness, for example, the thief on the cross or the man who came through the roof to be healed. On top of not asking, none had any shedding of blood to be forgiven. Blood is required by the old law (Leviticus 17:11) and the new covenant (Hebrews 9:22) as part of forgiveness, so how did they receive forgiveness? If you have to ask this question, then you may be forgetting who Jesus is and the two parts of forgiveness. Jesus is and always has been God the Son. The blood is there to heal the separation between man and God, but those who were in physical contact with Him did not need a blood sacrifice to be able to be at His feet. They had God with them and could ask and/or receive forgiveness firsthand. Jesus often forgave people because of their great faith (Luke 5:20) and love (Luke 7:47-48) for Him. Even with Abraham, the Bible never tells us that it is through confession but faith that caused Abraham to be righteous (Genesis 15:6) in His eyes. God can forgive in many ways, but in each of these unique instances of forgiveness, they approached the Lord with humility, faith, and love for who Jesus is, or found it in their encounter with Him. Remember that all sins are against God personally, so He can forgive sins against Himself even if not asked. The king of any kingdom has full authority over what goes on and can forgive when He sees fit (Matthew 18:21-35). Why not do this all the time? This would require a few things

- First - Jesus would have to remain here on earth and to meet everyone one-on-one. This would also mean that there would be no Holy Spirit because it was only after He left that man could be filled with the Spirit.
- Second, we would have to be better than we are. Through all the ages, God has dealt with man in so many ways, some of which were face-to-face, and man still rejected Him. God can see our hearts and knows this system is the best one for receiving the perfect bride. We see this rejection or dishonor of God not only in past ages but during the life of Jesus. He would heal people, and they would take what they received and return to their lives without following Him (Luke 17:11-19)

Jesus made the path to find forgiveness through the act of His grace and our obedience to believe and confess to receive forgiveness no matter when or where we are. He created the perfect situation to bring out His perfect bride. This is what will work for us, and if we humble ourselves and be obedient to Him in what He has asked, we can be part of His bride, and He will make us perfect before the Father.

The Bride Price

Jesus paid the price not just for our forgiveness; He wanted something in return. Jesus' blood also paid the bride price for us. All who are willing to accept His gift of salvation convert into a part of the Church and, therefore, become His betrothed. He has sealed His betrothal with the Holy Spirit, and part of our salvation is the inward dwelling of the Holy Spirit. A higher bride price has never been paid than our Lord God giving Himself to be the payment. His arrangements are in order, and He is knocking at mankind's door. if we are willing, He will come to build a relationship with us and then, one way or another, collect us into His kingdom.

1 Corinthians 6:19-20 (NKJV) - Or do you not know that your body is a temple of the Holy Spirit within you, whom you have from God? You are not your own, for you were bought with a price. So glorify God in your body.

The Work of the Church

Over the last 2,000 years, God has given his church His new covenant to live by. This new covenant is obeying the moral law in new ways, some even stricter than the old, but in many ways, the new law makes it much easier to find redemption and forgiveness of trespasses. We are given more help through the Holy Spirit, and because of this help, God expects more out of us (James 3:1). There are laws in the Old Testament that say do not murder or commit adultery, but now, if you hate or lust, you have committed these things in your heart. All this is because we have the Holy Spirit in us, and He changes us from the inside out. You will be changed not by knowing the law but by submitting yourself to the Spirit in all things. Through submission, we no longer fulfill the lusts of the flesh. With this, we have advantages over all those who lived before us because of the inward dwelling of the Spirit. Therefore, with great advantage comes great responsibility.

The Church age started with the Twelve Apostles, also known as the Twelve Apostles of the Lamb. There have only been twelve since Paul took Judas' place.

Revelations 21:14 (ESV) - And the wall of the city had twelve foundations, and on them were the twelve names of the twelve apostles of the Lamb.

Many, even today, can still be called to the apostles' work through missionary work, teaching, and discipleship. The Greek word ἀπόστολος (apóstolos) means one who is sent off or with a message. Many people do the work of an apostle. However, only the 12 called by Jesus can be God's mouthpiece or Apostles of the Lord. What they declared to others became God's word for us. God worked mightily through these men, proving their placement. All but one died with the proclamation of Jesus on their lips and went to eternity through martyrdom. When Judas' soul was lost, God chose Paul to take his place (1 Corinthians 1:1)

Psalm 41:9-10 (KJV) - Yea, mine own familiar friend, in whom I trusted, Who did eat of my bread, Hath lifted up his heel against me. But thou, O Jehovah, have mercy upon me, and raise me up, That I may requite [restore] them.

This is the prophecy talked about in Acts 1:16. The requite in this verse is to restore the twelve. We can understand this is the words of David that Peter was talking about. They tried to fulfill it themselves with Mathias, but Jesus was the only one who could pick the apostles, and he chose Paul as the true successor. These Apostles set the world on fire for God; even though the principalities of the devil were fully armed and against their ministry, they persevered by the blood of the Lamb and the word of His testimony.

During this church age, we have had many great men rise up in ministries all the way to our present age. I would recommend that all people study the history of the Church. Learning from past successes and failures is always a good idea for moving forward in knowledge and confidence. Nonetheless, the mission and the truth are still the same today as they were 2,000 years ago. There is no less call on the Christians' lives today than the ones who physically saw him with their own eyes (Matthew 28:16-20)

The Closing of the Church

One day soon, when the trumpet sounds, Jesus will come back and gather together His people.

1 Thessalonians 4:13–18 (ESV) - But we do not want you to be uninformed, brothers, about those who are asleep, that you may not grieve as others do who have no hope. For since we believe that Jesus died and rose again, even so, through Jesus, God will bring with him those who have fallen asleep. For this we declare to you by a word from the Lord, that we who are alive, who are left until the coming of the Lord, will not precede those who have fallen asleep. For the Lord himself will descend heaven with a cry of command, with the voice of an archangel, and with the sound of the trumpet of God. And the dead in Christ will rise first. Then we who are alive, who are left, will be caught up together with them in the clouds to meet the Lord in the air, and so we will always be with the Lord. Therefore, encourage one another with these words. (Also see John 14:3, Revelation 3:10, Philippians 3:20-21, 1 Corinthians 15:50-53, 1 Thessalonians 4:13-18, Luke 17:34-37)

This is the fulfillment of the word of Jesus that He is coming for His Bride, the Church. Since the time of the cross, Jesus has been bearing the sins of the world to re-establish man's connection to the Father so they can find forgiveness through confession. This storing of sins, however, has been building up wrath against mankind at the same time.

1 John 2:2 (KJV) - And He Himself is the propitiation for our sins, and not for ours only but also for the whole world.

Since Jesus took upon Himself the sins of the whole world, two very contrasting things are happening.

1. Jesus died for our sins, and those who repent of their sins are forgiven. He casts them away far from us, never to be remembered again or used against us. They are fully

forgiven, and the wrath from those sins bears no further burden.

2. Jesus' burden of sacrifice was for the whole world, including those who did not repent. The unrepented sins of the lost are never resolved. These sins are being stored up wrath in the six bowls of judgment that will be poured on the earth (Revelation 16). When all the bowls are poured out, the Son will return. He will be here to conquer the Earth and fulfill the remaining prophecies about Himself.

The Rapture

Because thou hast kept the word of my patience, I also will keep thee from the hour of temptation, which shall come upon all the world, to try them that dwell upon the earth. (Revelation 3:10 KJV)

The word rapture is not in scripture; it is a word used to define the events that take place in the Bible. Some call it the great catching away or the first return of Christ. It is the end of the Church age and ends the search for His Bride. Once the rapture happens, those left will call out to God, but like those outside of Noah's Ark, there will be no one to save them from the trials that come next. While we anxiously await the Lord's return, we should be doing all we can in our kingdom's work, taking everything He has taught us and putting it into practice (Matthew 6:19-21).

Matthew 16:18 (ESV) - And I tell you, you are Peter, and on this rock I will build my church, and the gates of hell shall not prevail against it. (see also Colossians 1:26-27)

For the past nearly 2,000 years, the Church has not changed much. We are still on the mission that Jesus gave us, called the Great Commission. However, all things will begin to change at the moment of the rapture, when the Church He has established is taken out of this world. The rapture will set off a chain of events that will see the end of this world within a seven-year time span. We are close to this change of the age of Man.

John 14:3 (NKJV) - And if I go and prepare a place for you, I will come again and receive you to Myself; that where I am, there you may be also. (see also; Hebrews 9:27-28, Philippians 3:20-21, 1

Corinthians 15:50-53, 1 Thessalonians 4:13-18, Luke 17:34-37, Revelation 19:7-9)

Jesus will conquer all people; those who love Him will follow Him in complete submission as the Bride. The rest of the world will learn submission or become submissive through force. However, in the end, every knee will bow, and every tongue will confess that He is Lord (Philippians 2:10-11). The first part of His return, known as the rapture, will be apart from sin, meaning after this moment, He is no longer bearing or carrying our sins upon Him.

Hebrews 9:26-28 (ESV) - for then he would have had to suffer repeatedly since the foundation of the world. But as it is, he has appeared once for all at the end of the ages to put away sin by the sacrifice of himself. And just as it is appointed for man to die once, and after that comes judgment, so Christ, having been offered once to bear the sins of many, will appear a second time, not to deal with sin but to save those who are eagerly waiting for him.

At the moment of the rapture, Jesus no longer continues to carry our sins. From that point on, the way to redemption reverts to a way much closer to the Old Testament. We need to know that before Christ came, people could only go to hell or paradise. Heaven was out of reach, and after the rapture, it will revert to this way once again in many ways. There will be some saved in the rapture; these will need to have enough faith in God to die a martyr's death. They are not in a position where the blood of Christ on the Ark will cover them, nor will Jesus take their sins away to fulfill the righteousness of the law. The blood guilt will be paid by their martyr's death in faith. Those saved during the Tribulation will not join the Church for the marriage supper of the Lamb because they can no longer fulfill the law of righteousness. Instead, they will remain under the altar, calling out to God to take vengeance on the evil ones on Earth. Through the world's 7-year tribulation, all wrath that was stored up in the bowls of judgment for past sins of the world will be poured out. This is the last judgment and the beginning of the end of this 5th age; once again, the world will start a reset, and it's a sign that everything is about to change.

Never in human history has there been a stronger contrast between what is happening on Earth and what is happening in Heaven. On Earth, the seven years of tribulation will be the most unimaginable, horrific, and tragic time of suffering anyone has ever known. However, in Heaven, we will be in a seven-year celebration known as the marriage supper of the Lamb.

Revelation 19:6-9 (ESV) - Then I heard what seemed to be the voice of a great multitude, like the roar of many waters and like the sound of mighty peals of thunder, crying out, "Hallelujah! For the Lord our God the Almighty reigns. Let us rejoice and exult and give him the glory, for the marriage of the Lamb has come, and his Bride has made herself ready; it was granted her to clothe herself with fine linen, bright and pure"— for the fine linen is the righteous deeds of the saints. And the angel said to me, "Write this: Blessed are those who are invited to the marriage supper of the Lamb." And he said to me, "These are the true words of God."

We, as the church, will be witnessing Jesus opening the seals, releasing the horseman of the apocalypse, and other great and mighty prophecies that fulfill the words written in John's revelation. Then Jesus celebrates with us for 7 years. We sadly have very few spoilers for the Marriage Supper of the Lamb, other than the communion with our Lord. The feast itself, some songs, some gathering, and then we all prepare and return with Christ for the battle of Armageddon. The feast is the Church's long-awaited celebration with Jesus, and it will be amazing!

At the end of the tribulation, all the world will gather to fight against the Lord, and the Lord will once and for all end the conflict between man and God. At this point, the world will understand who God is and will mourn because they will realize they are fighting on the wrong side. It will end quickly as the Son fights and ends the battle of Armageddon Himself. This battle closes out the 5th age of our Earth.

Matthew 24:29-30 (NKJV) - "Immediately after the tribulation of those days the sun will be darkened, and the moon will not give its light; the stars will fall from heaven, and the powers of the heavens will be shaken. Then the sign of the Son of Man will appear in heaven, and then all the tribes of the earth will mourn, and they will see the Son of Man coming on the clouds of heaven with power and great glory. (also Revelation 19:11-21)

Quick Recap of this Chapter

- God's longing has always been to have a people. He can say, you are my people, and I will be your God.
- Through His Son, we are signed, sealed, and soon delivered.
- The first step of repentance is always open from that time forward, and we are born again into the covenant of Grace (John 3).
- Jesus washes our sins away, and the door to salvation remains open forever to those who accept Him.
- The blood covers us and no longer keeps us out of the presence of God, but sin can still overtake us if we allow it into our lives.
- Dying daily, as Paul taught us to do, is of the utmost importance to protect ourselves from falling away from the grace He supplied.
- Once we are reborn again, we become part of the Bride of Christ, which is better known as the Church.
- The Church has been waiting for Christ's return for the last 2000 years. We are seeing this time coming to a close
- At the end of the church, Christ will rapture us, starting a seven-year timer, much like the 120-year timer set in Noah's day. During these seven years, there will be judgment on the earth and the marriage supper of the Lamb in heaven.

Chapter 6
The Millennial Reign
&
The End of the
World

6th Age - The Millennial Kingdom

Then I saw an angel coming down from heaven, having the key to the bottomless pit and a great chain in his hand. He laid hold of the dragon, that serpent of old, who is the Devil and Satan, and bound him for a thousand years; and he cast him into the bottomless pit, and shut him up, and set a seal on him, so that he should deceive the nations no more till the thousand years were finished. But after these things, he must be released for a little while. - Revelation 20:1-3 (NKJV)

Things move quickly after the battle of Armageddon. After Satan's army is defeated at Armageddon, Lucifer is bound in prison for 1,000 years. Then, the long-awaited resurrection of Israel (Ezekiel 37), where all who are in Abraham's Bosom will be brought back to life to live in his new reign; this age will be Christ's rule on Earth as the King of Kings throughout the world. This is how it was intended in the Garden of Eden from the start. All individuals will return to human life. Marrying, working, and having children (Ezekiel 37:25-28), but they will have one supreme King Jesus that will rule over the world. Also, Israel will have David ruling as king of Israel at the world's epicenter. There will be kings who will rule all the other nations of the Earth. We are given some details about what life will be like. However, we are not given a specific timeframe for the life expectancy of those living during this age. The Bible does allude to a return to a long-life expectancy of roughly 1,000 years. This is taken from how long it appears David will be ruling. Following the course shown throughout the Bible, when godly kings are in power, the kingdom thrives, but after they pass and kings who don't have the same experiences take authority, the nations start to fall. The world will see 1,000 years of peace throughout the whole world. So, every nation will be run by people who love God. After the 1,000 years are over, people start to pull away from God, and God releases Satan back into the world. While the restored godly men rule, there is no war. After 1,000 years, the world falls into complete war. This gives the best evidence that man's life span will be around 1,000 years during this time.

In the last chapter, I mentioned that the place under the Alter and Abrahams bosom were one and the same, and here is why. First, we need to understand where the Information is coming from. In the book of Ezekiel, the prophecies are separated by the times Ezekiel received them.

Old Covenant

- Chapter 1-3 – Ezekiel's Calling
- Chapter 4 -24 – Judgement of Gods People
- Chapter 25-32 – Judgments of God's Enemies
- Chapter 33 – God's Presence Removed from Israel
  (Church Age skipped as Ezekiel is only writing for Israel to understand what God is doing for them and through them, but a majority of Israel rejected the wedding invitation Matthew 22:1-14)

Fulfillment of God's Promises to Israel in a 1,000-Year Reign

- Chapter 33-39 – Restoration and promises of Israel at the start of the 1,000-year reign, David set as King
- Chapter 40-48 – Description of Temple during the 1,000-year reign

Q) How do we know that Chapters 33 through 48 are during the 1,000-year reign?

- Firstly, there is the location of Jesus Himself. Jesus will not be on Earth until after the battle of Armageddon, but we see Him on Earth and physically living in the temple. There isn't a temple in the New Heaven and Earth, so it is pinpointed to this Age.

and he said to me, "Son of man, this is the place of my throne and the place of the soles of my feet, where I will dwell in the midst of the people of Israel forever. And the house of Israel shall no more defile my holy name, neither they, nor their kings, by their whoring and by the dead bodies of their kings at their high places, by setting their threshold by my threshold and their doorposts beside my doorposts, with only a wall between me and them. They have defiled my holy name by their abominations that they have committed, so I have consumed them in my anger. Now let them put away their whoring and the dead bodies of their kings far from me, and I will dwell in their midst forever.. - Ezekiel 43:7-9 (ESV)

- Secondly, John's revelation gives the timeline of the events that happened in Ezekiel.

And when the thousand years are ended, Satan will be released from his prison and will come out to deceive the nations that are at the four corners of the earth, Gog and Magog, to gather them for battle; their number is like the sand of the sea. And they marched up over the broad plain of the earth and surrounded the camp of the saints and the beloved city, but fire came down from heaven and consumed them, and the devil who had deceived them was thrown into the lake of fire and sulfur where the beast and the false prophet were, and they will be tormented day and night forever and ever.. – Revelation 20:7-10 (ESV)

- Thirdly, we are told this is the time of David's return and the Rule of Israel and the details of what He will be doing. (Ezekiel 34:23-24, Ezekiel 37:24-25)

Ezekiel chapters 33 – 39 are about the restoration of Israel and godly rule. Then, the world changes dramatically into chaos with the battle of Gog and Magog. Wood weapons will be used in this war mostly because they will be coming out of 1,000 years of peace and will have no weapons but the ones they fashioned right before they came to make war. All these weapons are primitive, such that when the battle is over, they will be turned into firewood. As of now, Israel has not been restored, even though most biblical teachers will teach that the prophecy of Israel has been accomplished (Ezekiel 36:24). However, when they are restored, both Judah and Ephraim, which is all Israel, not just Judah, will once again be made into one nation. All of Israel that has ever existed will be able to be resorted to one unified nation. Abraham, Isaac, and Jacob, along with every faithful Israelite, will be there to guide Israel into unity. United with Jesus as their King. Israel has not been a united nation since the time of Solomon, and during the 1,000-year reign, it will be once again.

Ezekiel 37:15-17 (KJV) - The word of Jehovah again came to me, saying: "And you, son of man, take a stick and write on it, 'For Judah and for the people of Israel who are with him.' Then take another stick and write on it, 'For Joseph, the stick of Ephraim, and all the house of Israel who are with him.' Then bring them close to each other so that they become just one stick in your hand.

Understanding Abraham's Bosom

We know that Israel and, for that matter, most of mankind have been waiting in a place known as paradise (Abraham's Bosom). This place is separate from the Father but also not in torment. It is a dedicated place for all people from Adam until the resurrection of the dead after the tribulation. If people have not been found guilty and awaiting judgment in hell or have passed on in the grace in agreement to the covenant of Jesus, then this is where their souls have been since their deaths.

- Those before the Law, because no sin was accounted to them.
- All those who knew the law and were faithful to it.
- Those who lived during the time of the law but did not receive the revelation of the law.

These people will fall into the same judgment as those born before the law existed. This also makes the point that those today who don't get a chance to know God will be in Abraham's bosom/Paradise, awaiting the resurrection. They will have the chance to accept or reject the Lord during the 1,000-year reign. To add to this further, the Bible also says plainly that Paradise (Abraham's Bosom) resides in the third heaven, where the Father dwells, but it is still separate from eternal life with the Father.

2 Corinthians 12:2-4 (ASV) - I know a man in Christ, fourteen years ago (whether in the body, I know not; or whether out of the body, I know not; God knoweth), such a one caught up even to the third heaven. And I know such a man (whether in the body, or apart from the body, I know not; God knoweth), how that he was caught up into Paradise, and heard unspeakable words, which it is not lawful for a man to utter.

Where paradise resides is made clear, but there is still a separation between God's dwelling and paradise. The awaiting souls are kept under the Altar of the Father, and Abraham is the keeper until the reign of Christ begins. I think of it as being at a theme park but stuck at the ticket counter in line—able to perhaps see but unable to participate. I say the souls may be able to see because of their calling out to the Father during the tribulation for vengeance (Revelation 6:10). This is not definite evidence that they can see into heaven, but it gives more reason to believe they can than to doubt it. There is a definite interaction between Heaven and paradise.

"Then they were each given a white robe and told to rest a little longer" - Revelations 6:11 (ESV), but to what extent we do not know.

Why am I spending this time detailing the workings of the place called Paradise (Abrahams Bosom)? The main reason is that, at the beginning of this age, it will be emptied out. Starting the 1,000-year reign. After it is emptied, it will begin to be the place for the dead to await the Great White Throne Judgment. The Bible tells us,

2 Corinthians 5:8 (KJV) - We are confident, I say, and willing rather to be absent from the body and to be present with the Lord.

Once we die, our souls do not reside in dead flesh but go into the spiritual realm. However, during the 1,000-year reign, there is an issue because the Lord will be on Earth living in the new temple.

Ezekiel 43:7-9 (NKJV) - and he said to me, "Son of man, this is the place of my throne and the place of the soles of my feet, where I will dwell in the midst of the people of Israel forever. And the house of Israel shall no more defile my holy name, neither they, nor their kings, ... Now let them put away their whoring and the dead bodies of their kings far from me, and I will dwell in their midst forever.

If Jesus is in the Temple, that would mean when someone dies during those 1,000+ years, their souls must go somewhere. Do keep in mind the punishment of hell is still open even though the devil is locked away. However, for the faithful to be absent from the body is to be present with the Lord; if this continues, then this would become a problem of ghosts wandering the earth everywhere. This has never been the way the Lord works. Keep in mind that the White Throne Judgment has not yet taken place, so they won't be able to have eternal life in heaven with the Father either. The best answer we have is that in the 1,000-year reign, those who die will go back to Abraham's bosom (which will take the name Death once again Revelation 20:13). People will die, and even some of Earth's largest wars will take place at the close of this age, especially the war of Gog and Magog. However, this time, since the entire world will be without the excuse of having the chance to know God, then once they die, they will await judgment in Hell or under the alter (paradise/Abraham's Bosom). All people will have enough knowledge to make their eternal choice without excuse.

The New and Old Mix

At the start of the 6th Age, over these 1,000 years, there will be numerous other changes. The covenant that Jesus established was completed. Much like when your husband or wife passes away, the wedding covenant is completed, and you are free to remarry if you desire. The earth will receive new laws and customs during this time, which will seem hard for many people from our current age to deal with. The return to animal sacrifices for sin will be re-established at the temple (Ezekiel 43:18-46:24, Isaiah 56:6-8, Zechariah 14:16, Jeremiah 33:15-18). People will bring their sacrifices and offerings to the lord; this includes offerings for sin. However, the yearly sacrifice in the Holy of Holies will not be needed since the presence of the Lord is with the people continually.

Ezekiel 43:18-27 (ESV) - ....And on the second day you shall offer a male goat without blemish for a sin offering; and the altar shall be purified, as it was purified with the bull....

This is not a full return to the time of Moses; it will be different in many ways, and for most people that will be on the earth at this time, it will be what they were accustomed to already doing: Their regular worship to the Lord. You must remember that those who are coming back to life during the 1,000 years are the same people who already did this on a regular basis, so for them, there is nothing abnormal about it. The ones who will find it strange are the tribulation saints who will be required to make these sacrifices. There will be one huge difference during this timeframe. There will be no Satan or demons at this time to pull people away from God. No one at the other end of the tug-a-war rope in their spiritual battle of good and evil. It will be just the Lord, and He will be visible for the world to see Him as well. That is not to say our flesh will not rebel, but the pressures and tricks of the devil will be eliminated for 1,000 years.

The Bible only mentioned Satan being bound for 1,000 years, but what about the other demons? If just Satan himself were bound, that wouldn't make too much of a difference. All the other demons who hate God would still be making havoc on the Earth. So, it is reasonable to assume that at the end of the Tribulation, all demons are bound as well, like those under the river Euphrates are at this moment (Revelation 9:14). We are not told if all the demons are cast into hell or stored somewhere else during the 6th age. However, we see peace on earth and no deception or war on earth until the 1,000 years are finished. Not only Satan but all demonic powers are put away for this time. This is a big shift from what we must deal with daily and what all people have dealt with since Eve and the serpent had their little talk.

You must also keep in mind that most of these souls that are coming to life have been around a very long time, some over 7,000 years, making sure that when they get their next chance, they will not mess up like before. I doubt Eve will give ear to Satan again about what God really means when He speaks. Will Sampson be revealing any more secrets? Will Arron be making another golden calf in God's very presence? It seems unmistakably clear that their time spent waiting and watching in Abraham Bosom will produce a mighty force who will vow never to disappoint God in any way ever again, no matter the cost. So not only will His presence be known and seen during this time of Jesus' reign on earth, but the cloud of witnesses will be unparalleled by anything else before. The earth will be repopulated during this time, but the truth and wisdom that will be passed onto these little ones from all these people of old will simply be amazing. Imagine being able to sit and learn from Solomon, Job, Isaiah, Daniel, and even Adam himself. Not only all this but being ruled by David as the King of Israel!

If that last line caught you off guard, don't worry it is often missed as well. However, during the 1,000-year reign, David will once again be king and rule over the people of Israel. This makes not only logical sense but also fulfills many prophecies. The Son of God will be in the Temple, and He will remain in the Temple during the entirety of the 1,000 years. There will still need to be someone who will attend to kingdom matters and deal with the other lands that will have to work with Israel and make sure the accommodations are prepared so that all the nations of the world will be able to come and worship God in the new Jerusalem. With all of Israel brought back to life, think about who God will choose to fill this position. Of course, the obvious answer is King David.

David as King

Ezekiel 37:22-28 (KJV) - And I will make them one nation in the land, on the mountains of Israel. And one king shall be king over them all, and they shall be no longer two nations, and no longer divided into two kingdoms. They shall not defile themselves anymore with their idols and their detestable things, or with any of their transgressions. But I will save them from all the backslidings in which they have sinned, and will cleanse them; and they shall be my people, and I will be their God. "My servant David shall be king over them, and they shall all have one shepherd. They shall walk in my rules and be careful to obey my statutes. They shall dwell in the land that I gave to my servant Jacob, where your fathers lived. They and their children and their children's children shall dwell there forever, and David my servant shall be their prince forever.

Hosea 3:4-5 (ASV) - For the children of Israel shall abide many days without king, and without prince, and without sacrifice, and without pillar, and without ephod or teraphim: afterward shall the children of Israel return, and seek Jehovah their God, and David their king, and shall come with fear unto Jehovah and to his goodness in the latter days.

Keep this in mind next time you read through the Bible, especially when you read about the throne of Israel. When God spoke to David, He said, *"Your house and your kingdom shall be established forever before you. Your throne shall be established* forever." *(1 Samuel 7:16 NKJV)*. It is not just Israel's throne, but it remains David's, and that makes it possible for David to sit once again on it. David is also given special rights to be the Prince of Israel. The title is now held by the Arch Angel Micheal (Daniel 10:13, 10:21, 12:1). Micheal was one of many but is the greatest. David now also holds this title and is allowed to be the only one allowed at the East gate to meet and eat with God there.

Ezekiel 44:3 (NKJV) - As for the prince, because he is the prince, he may sit in it to eat bread before the LORD; he shall enter by way of the vestibule of the gateway, and go out the same way."

I will consider a theory at this time since Micheal is the greatest prince of Israel, just as David will be. We are reminded that there are other princes with similar roles. Therefore, we will probably be seeing other prominent figures take on roles during this time as well. Maybe Sampson will be the chief of police, or maybe Solomon will be the one over education. **It is definitely not in scripture, and this is only theoretical**. Yet, it's still fun to think of what might be. What is in scripture is David coming to be known as the prince of Israel (Ezekiel 34:23-24), raised to the same position as the archangel Micheal in honor and position (Daniel 12:1).

Life in the 1,000–Year Reign

The Lord will also establish Israel as the center of the world at this time. God has promised Israel the land from the Nile to the Euphrates River, which will be their possession.

Genesis 15:18 (ESV) - On that day the LORD made a covenant with Abram, saying, "To your offspring I give this land, from the river of Egypt to the great river, the river Euphrates".

This will include parts of Israel and possibly a good majority of current Saudi Arabia. It will need to be a significant size because of the vast number of people it will contain. All of God's chosen people will live there from the time of Abraham onward. Then, the rest that comes out from under the altar will be given to the rest of the world to inhabit. This will be after the tribulation and battle of Armageddon, so it will not be a displacement of people's homes but a new border as the world's boundaries is made new. All people will stay close to Israel because everyone will be making trips there. Life will be simple; there will be no war or weapons during this time. Life will be good, and if issues arise, they can be handled by the Lord Himself.

We, as the Church, have a role to play as well. We will be the messengers and workers at this time. The word angels in the Bible has a very specific meaning. In Hebrew and Greek, it means "messenger." When we review all we have gone over and see that there are many worlds before and after our own, and the servants of God are helpers and messengers to God after their own time, we can finally get a true picture of what and who angels are.

Revelation 5:10 (NKJV) - And have made us kings and priests to our God; And we shall reign on the earth."

1 Corintians 6:1-3 (ESV) - When one of you has a grievance against another, does he dare go to law before the unrighteous instead of the saints? Or do you not know that the saints will judge the world? And if the world is to be judged by you, are you incompetent to try trivial cases? Do you not know that we are to judge angels? How much more, then, matters pertaining to this life!

In this Millennial Kingdom, we will serve God as priests and judges and have roles in the Kingdom, all of which involve being messengers (angels) to the High King, who is Jesus. This does not mean we will be in the same form as the angels of our current age. We might, we might not; the Bible does not allude to this in any way. Nonetheless, we will serve in the same way that angels serve. There will be many Kingdom roles, just as the angels of Heaven do now for us. God is just, and everyone gets to live and make their choice to serve God or reject Him. Then, in the next world, we will serve God as messengers. If all things follow the same order, after our service is complete, we will be replaced by those chosen from the world we serve. At that point, we will leave to dwell with the Father forever. This is a privilege and an honor I am very much looking forward to.

The role of those who come from a previous world helps explain demons in many ways; for example, there are many similarities between what happened to Lucifer's world and our world at the end of each one, especially with Gog and Magog. Lucifer led a rebellion against God. As seen in the vision of Revelation 12, 1/3 of the angels fell because they sided with Lucifer against the Lord. Fast forward to the war after the 1,000 years have ended, about 1/3 of the earth will fall once again.

Q: How do we know 1/3 of the earth will fall in Gog's battle?

Noah had three sons: Japheth, Ham, & Shem. Japheth sons were *Gomer, Magog, Madai, Javan, Tubal, Meshek, and Tiras* (Genisis 10:2). When you compare that to the ones Gog will lead into battle after the 1,000 years of peace in Ezekiel 38, you will see that of Noah's descendants about 1/3 of them joined by Persia, Cush, and Put, come to make war on God.

Q: What connections are there from the old world and the current world?

In Lucifer's time, 1/3 of the inhabitants fell, and again, in our current world's future, 1/3 of the inhabitants will fall once again. This is reasoning by scripture, but if these events align perfectly, I suppose that David will be taking Michael's place, and Gog will be taking Lucifer's place on the next Earth. This might be spot on or not be the case at all. Nevertheless, it is a remarkable similarity. Interestingly, Lucifer was not ever referred to as an angel but rather a cherub in the Bible (Ezekiel 28:14). Any guess about past events, including who Lucifer was, is futile, so that doesn't help us piece this together any further. There is also an infinite number of possibilities for future events that could take place. I only mention this because it seems the most plausible, and I urge you to take this portion with a grain of salt. The devil has a long past and a short future, much like Gog will have. In the New Heaven and Earth, people will fail again so that a tempter may be necessary. This is because free will dictates that there can always be someone or something that opposes God. This ensures there is always a choice and decision to serve God in every life. Even in the

1,000-year reign, no demonic forces will be at work. Yet, Man retains the sinful nature to go against God from fleshly desires; Man would become His own enemy and must find forgiveness for that rebellion through animal sacrifice. During these future ages, no one opposes God face-to-face more than Gog, nor does anyone fit in Lucifer's shoes better than Gog, a man picked by Lucifer to lead the revolt after his release from prison.

Battle of Gog

Looking at the scriptures plainly, Gog is a man from the land of Magog (Ezekiel 38 – 39, Revelations 20). We know nothing else about his background besides his name, where he is from, and His title as leader and prince of lands. After 1,000 years of peace, Gog will be enticed by the freshly released Satan. There are some details we are told about this. Israel will treat the Lord with contempt once again, causing the protection of the Lord to be lifted and Satan to be released back onto the Earth (Ezekiel 39:17-29). After Gog is enticed, they gather the lands around them and prepare for battle. Gathering the lands is probably the time that weapons are beginning to be made for war. All modern weapons will be nonexistent. They will be bringing with them their fashioned swords, shields, bucklers, clubs, bows, and spears (Ezekiel 38 & 39, Revelation 20:8-9).

Such a great army will march from the North; Magog most likely inhabits the area of current Russia because the ancient name of Magog has its roots in Russian territory. The armies will most likely assemble above the Euphrates River and start the march south into Israel's land. God will defeat them, and it will take 7 months for them to bury all the bodies. They will also have enough firewood from weapons alone to last for 7 years. The Lord will let some destruction happen to Israel because of their rebellion. There will be many taken captive, and after the battle, they that have been taken to foreign lands will be brought back. Not one person will be left as a captive in enemy territory (Ezekiel 39:9-16).

2 Peter 3:7-10 (ESV) - But by the same word the heavens and earth that now exist are stored up for fire, being kept until the day of judgment and destruction of the ungodly. But do not overlook this one fact, beloved, that with the Lord one day is as a thousand years and a thousand years as one day. The Lord is not slow to fulfill his promise as some count slowness, but is patient toward you, not wishing that any should perish, but that all should reach repentance. But the day of the Lord will come like a thief, and then the heavens will pass away with a roar, and the heavenly bodies will be burned up and dissolved, and the earth and the works that are done on it will be exposed.

As you read these verses in connection with all the other information we have, you can realize that the first 1,000 years are a day of rest, so the world, hypotactically, may very well go on 6,000 years, more or less. These years are past the time of the events revealed to us in the Bible. It will be a different time, but remember what God told us.

1 Corinthians 2:9-10 (ESV) - But, as it is written, "What no eye has seen, nor ear heard, nor the heart of man imagined, what God has prepared for those who love him"— these things God has revealed to us through the Spirit.

There is so much we still don't know; sometime in the future, we will get to walk with the Lord and live it out. Whenever the end comes, events will mark the Earth for destruction. These events will put all things under Jesus's feet. He will have no adversaries left on the face of the Earth. Then, at this point, the Son will hand the Kingdom of Heaven back to the Father. The Father will come to the world, and the world with all its elements will melt and flee away from the face of the Father. All will stand before the Father, and there they will have eternal judgment pronounced on every individual.

1 Corinthians 15:24-26 (ESV) - Then comes the end, when he delivers the kingdom to God the Father after destroying every rule and every authority and power. For he must reign until he has put all his enemies under his feet. The last enemy to be destroyed is death.

The Souls of the Departed

One oversight is often overlooked when considering the changes of the ages. I wanted to go over it before we move on to the new world. Think about what will happen to our bodies and souls during our deaths and when we enter the next stages of existence.

- For those who are raptured are changed into a new spiritual body, and our souls remain in the same place. Our bodies go through the change, but the soul never has to leave the body. It just experiences the changes as it happens.

- Those who have died as Christians and go to be with the Lord remain as only souls. Then, they come back with God during the rapture. The graves open up as the dead in Christ are raised first (1 Thessalonians 4:16-17). They are rejoined with their bodies, or their bodies are made anew because some will be ashes, and some will be dust. Then, all at the same time, they will be changed into a new spiritual body, and their souls will enter into their new bodies, ready for eternity

- Everyone who has died prior to Jesus or has never had the opportunity to follow Jesus has existed only as a soul. They have been without a physical or spiritual body since the time of their deaths. Those before Jesus' resurrection are not part of the body of Christ, so they are not the bride of Christ and will remain in Abraham's bosom until the start of the 1,000-year reign. This means some souls have been waiting about 7,000 years. Souls are capable of limited actions on their own. If you look at the story of Saul calling Samuel from Abraham's bosom. Samuel could talk with Saul but was only visible to the woman who called him. The soul is in an eternal state, is self-aware, and feels pain and thirst (Luke 16:24). No physical or spiritual body is needed, and the soul alone, although limited, can know what is happening around it. We also see in 1 Samuel 28 that Samuel retained all His memories and looks, including his age. The rich man retained who he was but was in hell and yet was in a state of torment, which he tried to get relief from Lazarus. When people return to Earth after the tribulation, they will have mortal physical bodies once again to live or reject God during their life in the 1,000-year reign.

- Those who die in sin against God and have been placed in hell are there from the time of their deaths until the day of the White Throne Judgment.
- Everyone who is not in hell and is residing under the altar (Abraham's bosom) will be raised back into life and living during the 1,000-year reign will have mortal bodies for a time, and everyone will be given a chance to follow or reject God. They will die at some point and wait until judgment, once again staying under the altar until the day of judgment. We are never given a time when they are given an eternal spiritual body, and they may wait until the judgment is passed to receive it. Then, after judgment, those who receive eternal life would receive their spiritual bodies and enter eternity with the Father. Nevertheless, those going to hell whose names are not found in the Book of Life are sent to hell, more than likely as just souls forever.
- The only ones that the Bible gives the precise times when people will get a glorified eternal spiritual body are those who are the bride of Christ. Those who accept Jesus as their Lord and Savior.

1 Corinthians 15:53-55 (KJV) - For this corruptible must put on incorruption, and this mortal must put on immortality. So when this corruptible shall have put on incorruption, and this mortal shall have put on immortality, then shall be brought to pass the saying that is written, Death is swallowed up in victory.

Those in Christ will be glorified and never fear death. That is the second death of Hell. We will live forever and reign with our Lord and Savior.

Chapter 7
New Heaven and Earth

7th Age - New Heaven and Earth

The New Heaven and Earth is a surprising look into what the next Earth and life on it will be like. As we discussed in previous chapters, the dwelling of the Father in the 3rd Heaven is an eternal kingdom that does not change. The new creation happens in a new space within our universe. The earth will have new heavens, which are the 1st and 2nd heavens (sky and galaxy). In this new galaxy, the new earth will be created with new people. These newly created people will be working on being the new bride of Christ by remaining pure and honorable before the Lord (Revelation Ch 21-22). On this earth, the Son will set up a new garden, where He will freely dwell with man as He intended with Adam and Eve. If we were to compare the 6th age with the 7th age, we would notice some strong contrasts.

- During the 6th age (the 1,000-year reign), Jesus was showing us how a noble king should have ruled. Nonetheless, people still possessed their sinful natures, and there was still evil in the world. The Earth itself continued groaning with pain (Romans 8:22). Animals will still kill and eat each other, and peace will still be worked on. This is because the sinful nature from the original fall stays with man as long as the Earth remains.

- In the 7th age, when the Father melts away all of the Earth and heavens, the original fall is conquered and destroyed, and with all things under the Son's feet, gives the kingdom of Heaven back to the Father. Merging the Kingdom of Heaven with the Kingdom of God, at this point, there will be no more sinful nature inside of His creation. With the new creation, people will have the chance not to fall, and it seems this next Earth will make better choices than ours did. After a while, some of the new creations will fall, but not all of them. There will be a split within mankind, some who wholly keep God's commands and those who fall away. People will live and die, but their lifespans will be like trees, to the point that someone who dies at only 100 years old will still be considered too young to die or die accursed because they sinned. The animals will live together in peace and not eat each other. There will be no need for a temple because He will dwell openly with His people.

Isaiah 65:17-25 (KJV) - For, behold, I create new heavens and a new earth: and the former shall not be remembered, nor come into mind. But be ye glad and rejoice for ever in that which I create: for, behold, I create Jerusalem a rejoicing, and her people a joy. And I will rejoice in Jerusalem, and joy in my people: and the voice of weeping shall be no more heard in her, nor the voice of crying. There shall be no more thence an infant of days, nor an old man that hath not filled his days: for the child shall die an hundred years old; but the sinner being an hundred years old shall be accursed. And they shall build houses, and inhabit them; and they shall plant vineyards, and eat the fruit of them. They shall not build, and another inhabit; they shall not plant, and another eat: for as the days of a tree are the days of my people, and mine elect shall long enjoy the work of their hands. They shall not labour in vain, nor bring forth for trouble; for they are the seed of the blessed of the Lord, and their offspring with them. And it shall come to pass, that before they call, I will answer; and while they are yet speaking, I will hear. The wolf and the lamb shall feed together, and the lion shall eat straw like the bullock: and dust shall be the serpent's meat. They shall not hurt nor destroy in all my holy mountain, saith the Lord. (Also see Revelation 21:1-27)

There will be a fraction of people on the new earth, nations that walk with God and those that don't. Those who do these detestable things will be alienated from the glorious city, reminiscent of the fall of Adam and Eve.

Revelation 21:24-27 (ESV) - By its light will the nations walk, and the kings of the earth will bring their glory into it, and its gates will never be shut by day—and there will be no night there. They will bring into it the glory and the honor of the nations. But nothing unclean will ever enter it, nor anyone who does what is detestable or false, but only those who are written in the Lamb's book of life.

The righteous ones of the city shall be able to go out and look at those who rebel against the Lord. They shall be dead and can be seen as a remembrance of what rebelling against the Lord brings. (Isaiah 66:22-24). Keep in mind that our world was utterly destroyed, and all the elements melted away. (2 Peter 3:12). These dead bodies Isaiah is talking about are from God's newly created beings. In the new Earth, there will be those who choose to disobey God. God allows this because He still wants true followers and true worship, not robotic obedience. Those people who choose sin will be cast out of God's presence and not allowed back into the new Jerusalem. This shows that this world will have fallen people but will also have those who stay righteous and do not fall away during their lives. Their worldly existence will be spent with God each and every day, and when they pass away, they will be part of His new bride. These righteous people of the new Earth will live lives similar to Jesus' earthly life as far as obedience to the Father and will go directly to be with the Father after their celebrated passing.

The new world will have night and day, a new sun and moon (Or perhaps a completely different type of solar system). However, inside the city itself, there will be no night. The Lord will dwell openly there, and the Son Himself will be the light of the new

Jerusalem. We are only given a small glimpse into the life of the New Earth and Heavens and not told much else. We don't have knowledge of what roles there will be or the details of this new creation. I can tell you this: it will be amazing to watch it unfold.

One thing I find interesting is that we, in our current age, get just a small glimpse of the world that came before our own. The new world will be the same as well. They will get a slice of knowledge of our world, such as the Apostle's names being written on the foundation of the New Jerusalem (Revelations 21:14). Most of our history will be erased, but fragments will remain (Isaiah 65:17, 66:22). There will be the children of the Lord from the 1,000-year reign who will remain on the new Earth to serve as the new messengers. As we said before, the cycle repeats over and over again.

Sin Nature

In the new world, the mindset of God's new creation will revert to the time before Adam and Eve ate the fruit from the Tree of Knowledge. To understand what the future will be like, we need to investigate our past. After Adam and Eve ate the fruit, man's sinful nature entered the world.

Ephesians 2:3 (ESV) - Among whom we all once lived in the passions of our flesh, carrying out the desires of the body and the mind, and were by nature children of wrath, like the rest of mankind.

When we are born, we are born with a sinful nature. However, sometimes, the sinful nature within us is misunderstood. Even Jesus had this sinful nature within Himself yet was without sin. I will prove this to you. When we are born, we are born innocent and without sin. In order to sin, you have to know that something is wrong and transgress in that manner. It can also be knowing to do good and not to do it. We, as Christians, need to work actively on this. When we are born, we are born pure, and Luke 17:2 sternly warns anyone who would guide children to lose that innocence. Rather, the sinful nature in us is the innate desire to fulfill fleshly desires.

When Adam and Eve sinned, a change in their minds happened. Think about it as if our minds were a USB flash drive. God created them, and their minds were plugged into the His Kingdom. Their thoughts and goals were instinctively based on what God wanted and His ways. They were very intelligent and still possessed free will, but all they wanted was from the Lord because their minds were focused on God. An example of this would be trying to talk a one-year-old into giving you candy they possessed for a five-dollar bill. The one-year-old is able to make their own choices but has no use for money and will not want to give up the candy for it. Their mindset is established into what they know, and they want nothing to do with the paper money you are offering.

Then the serpent came in with his talk and got Eve to eat the fruit. At this moment, the sinful nature did not take effect because it was not God's command of Eve not to eat the fruit but Adam's. However, when Adam was convinced by Eve to eat it, a large shift happened in their minds. Like a virus entering their hearts and minds. It was like the metaphorical UBS sticks of their minds were yanked out of the kingdom mindset and plugged into the world. A world now fallen and cursed because of the sin they just committed. They lost not only their God-centered mental condition but their soul-acquired sin, which separated them from the presence of God as well.

Adam and Eve's minds were no longer connected to God as they had been before, but their eyes were opened to what their flesh desired and the shame of what their hands had done. In the New World, people's minds will be continually dwelling on the ways of God. They will be able to serve God out of natural reactions rather than sinning out of natural reactions. The Earth and the animals will be at peace. Peace will remain on earth for all those who continue to serve the Lord. There is a chance of falling, but it will be quite different from our world. Without the sinful nature, it is harder to sin. It's like playing tug-a-war with no one on the other side of the rope. While we have our sinful nature, our minds are pulled from what the flesh wants and what our God-given soul wants (1 Peter 2:11). That does not mean we can't be enticed by outside forces like Eve and the snake, but our minds are not at war with God, rather its focus is God. Jesus was tempted to sin by the devil. The devil knew that even though the soul of God was in a fleshly body, Jesus still had the mind of a man, which included a sinful nature. Jesus was made like us in every way to be a perfect high priest (Hebrews 2:17). Going through what we go through in life and being tempted with sin just as we are tempted. Jesus proved to us that just because we have a sinful nature inside of us does not mean we have to listen to it. Jesus was able to reject and spiritually battle the enemy using His firm foundation of the Word of God. We need to follow this exact example and overcome sin *"through the blood of the lamb and the word of His testimony"* (Revelation 12:11).

Chapter 8
What is Love

For Christians, there probably is no more important word to define than love. That is because God is love:

1 John 4:7-21 (ESV) - Beloved, let us love one another, for love is from God, and whoever loves has been born of God and knows God. Anyone who does not love does not know God, because God is love. In this the love of God was made manifest among us, that God sent his only Son into the world, so that we might live through him. In this is love, not that we have loved God but that he loved us and sent his Son to be the propitiation for our sins. Beloved, if God so loved us, we also ought to love one another. No one has ever seen God; if we love one another, God abides in us and his love is perfected in us. By this we know that we abide in him and he in us, because he has given us of his Spirit. And we have seen and testify that the Father has sent his Son to be the Savior of the world. Whoever confesses that Jesus is the Son of God, God abides in him, and he in God. So we have come to know and to believe the love that God has for us. God is love, and whoever abides in love abides in God, and God abides in him. By this is love perfected with us, so that we may have confidence for the day of judgment, because as he is so also are we in this world. There is no fear in love, but perfect love casts out fear. For fear has to do with punishment, and whoever fears has not been perfected in love. We love because he first loved us. If anyone says, "I love God," and hates his brother, he is a liar; for he who does not love his brother whom he has seen cannot love God whom he has not seen. And this commandment we have from him: whoever loves God must also love his brother.

If God is love, then our relationship with God is in part determined by how we love our brothers. This means our relationship and standing with the Lord will be based on our true definition and following of the word love. This four-letter word defines not only our doctrines and thoughts about the Lord but also how God sees us. We use love in so many ways: we love God, we love our spouse, we love our children, we love cheeseburgers, parks, and the type of flooring we put into our homes. We can use this word for so many things, but if we fail to understand the word itself, then we can never be ready to truly love God or one another. Nevertheless, God has made it simple for us. There is one definition that truly captures the definition of love. Love is simply **a state of readiness**.

We can be in a state of readiness for so many things.

- For our spouse, we can be ready to care for and support them as Christ was ready to care for and support the Church.
- For our children, we are ready to protect, financially support, and sacrifice for them.
- For a cheeseburger, we are ready to eat and enjoy it.
- You can love a particular flooring for your house so much that nothing else but the one you chose will do, and you are not "ready" to accept another type.

You get the idea that we can love so many things in so many ways and on so many levels. Our readiness to support and protect our children is on a much larger scale than your readiness to eat a cheeseburger. However, you can love both because of your readiness to work and put effort into these things. When the Bible says, *"he who does not love his brother whom he has seen cannot love God whom he has not seen" (1 John 4:20 NKJV).* It gives us a direct look at what will happen during the Great White Throne Judgment.

Matthew 25:31-46 (KJV) - ...And the King shall answer and say unto them, Verily I say unto you, inasmuch as ye have done it unto one of the least of these my brethren, ye have done it unto me. Then shall he say also unto them on the left hand, Depart from me, ye cursed, into everlasting fire, prepared for the devil and his angels: For I was an hungered, and ye gave me no meat: I was thirsty, and ye gave me no drink: I was a stranger, and ye took me not in, naked, and ye clothed me not: sick, and in prison, and ye visited me not.... And these will go away into eternal punishment, but the righteous into eternal life."

We must be ready to serve God by serving our brothers. We must be in a state of readiness to help those in need, caring for them as Christ would have done for them. This will stretch our idea of how we must treat our spouses. We believe that "love" in our marriages involves an emotional state. Even though emotions are attached to any relationship, to love something, especially someone, we must come to the realization that love is a state of readiness to act out in those relationships. Many times, our emotions quickly get us to the point of readiness, but a willingness to serve God fully or to uphold a vow we have taken can get us to the same state of readiness and be sustainable. Furthermore, if the love in our marriage is built on more than emotions, we can live out our lives with the one and only that we said "I do" with instead of quitting halfway through. As Christians, if you say you are unwilling to love your spouse, or for that fact, your mother, father, child, friend, or enemy, then you fall right back into the judgment found in Matthew 25 or many other passages that speak about neglecting our duties to one another.

In order to love, physical actions are required. It's "doing," not an emotional state. When you understand love, you can take the necessary steps to walk the path that God has set out for us. Truly wanting to serve God puts us in a state of readiness and helps us not react with vengeance but with compassion. It puts us in a state to do well to those who do hateful things to us, fulfilling the law of God.

Luke 6:27 (NKJV) - "But I say to you who hear, Love your enemies, do good to those who hate you."

How are We to Get Into a State of Readiness?

The main goal in Christians' lives should be to take the Word of God and let it guide our every action, in good times or bad. This means we need to know what it says. If we don't know what is in the Word, we cannot act or react in situations the way God has called us to do it. When Jesus was in the wilderness, He did not rely on his intelligence, morals, or upbringing to get him through it. He relied on the Word of God and fought the enemy through Scripture. Jesus let the scriptures dictate His actions when temptation came upon Him. Having the Word in our hearts and at the tip of our tongues is necessary to be like Christ. The Bible teaches us so many things in how we are to walk daily and prepare ourselves. If we apply these things, we will be well on our way to reaching our goal of being like Christ.

Another goal for the Christian is learning to lean hard on the Holy Spirit for direction and strength. Again, this is what Jesus did when walking with us in the flesh. Even if we can memorize the entire Bible word for word and know what to do in each and every situation, our flesh can get in the way, causing us to fail to apply what we know. This is where submitting to the Holy Spirit comes in. Knowledge is great, but without the Spirit to implement our knowledge into our lives, we will end up failing anyway. Knowledge alone will not prepare us to love. Only a willing heart that is ready to act can prepare you to be ready in all situations to be like Christ. The more we rely on the Holy Spirit, the less we will listen to our flesh when it wants to be selfish.

1 Corinthians 13:2 (ASV) - And if I have the gift of prophecy, and know all mysteries and all knowledge; and if I have all faith, so as to remove mountains, but have not love, I am nothing.

One last goal for the Christian is that readiness to help must be sincere. It's not about apathy or feelings but your readiness to act and then try to carry that action out till the end.

You can plan to visit those in prison for years on end but never make the drive. Loving is not about desires but sincerity so that when it comes time to act, you quickly move and walk toward that goal. Whether the situation contains a spontaneous or planned action, pulling the trigger on our physical and emotional actions is what matters. It's the "doing" that carries out love.

Our love is action-based and a state of our heart. When Jesus was asking Peter if He loved Him, he asked three times. The first two times were ἀγαπάω (agape) and an unconditional readiness to do the Lord's will. Peter responded with "φιλέω" (phileo), which is to be ready to love like a brother or friend. So, when Peter was unwilling to take on the readiness of unconditional surrender, and he asked him the 3ʳᵈ time do you love (phileo) me, Peter became sad, understanding He was limiting what he was willing to do in his relationship with Jesus. Like I said before, you can love on different levels. Parental love is one of our best ways to understand God's love. If there is a choice involving protecting your child, everything else, even our lives, is meaningless. This type of love is limitless. It's the unconditional love or readiness of the heart that Jesus wanted from Peter and from us as well.

Love of God

Our Love is a readiness of our heart, and it is the same for God. However, God's love also takes on another characteristic that we are incapable of producing. This is because oftentimes, our very nature is not to love. We can choose not to love, casting off our readiness for selfishness, self-preservation, or many other countless reasons our minds can come up with. God, on the other hand, can no more cast-off love than we can stop being human. It is in our nature to be human; it is the way God has created us to be, and there is no power we possess that can stop us from being human. That is what it means for something to be in your nature. The thing is built into your very being. We can choose to be in love or out of love. We can choose to hate or hurt as much as love. When your spouse wakes you up in the morning, and you decide to kiss or slap them, it is a choice that is made, not an inherent characteristic that defines us. As we said before, God is an entirely different being than ourselves, remembering that His soul (all that makes God Himself) is present in the Father. Then, it was passed into our reality through His Son, as well as spiritual reality through the Holy Spirit. They all contain God's soul, but our soul only came from the breath of God entering man. This means our created form or soul will not match the Trinity's.

We have inherited characteristics such as a portion of faith and being made in the image of God, but intrinsic love is not one of them. God's love is not something He does but is part of who He is. God has certain immutable characteristics, and to do the contrary would be the same as denying Himself. This would be in the same way as us stopping to be human. God has told us that He can't deny Himself (2 Timothy 2:13). Therefore, it is impossible to do certain things contrary to His own nature. God is flawless, unchanging, beyond ordinary experience, not bound by physical form, all-knowing, everywhere at once, capable of forming relationships, autonomous, perfectly just, infinitely compassionate, the originator of the universe, and important to this section, infinitely loving. Love is not what He does but who He is. Some might wonder where things like morality come from, and the answer is from the very nature of God. Knowing this gives us the insight that sin comes from the opposite of these aspects. Here is where some confusion comes in because the Bible says that God hates.

Proverbs 6:16-19 (ASV) - There are six things that the Lord hates, seven that are an abomination to him: haughty eyes, a lying tongue, and hands that shed innocent blood, a heart that devises wicked plans, feet that make haste to run to evil, a false witness who breathes out lies, and one who sows discord among brothers.

Psalm 11:5 (ESV) - The Lord tests the righteous, but his soul hates the wicked and the one who loves violence.

Malachi 1:2-3 (ESV) - "I have loved you," says the Lord. But you say, "How have you loved us?" "Is not Esau Jacob 's brother?" declares the Lord. "Yet I have loved Jacob, but Esau I have hated. I have laid waste his hill country and left his heritage to jackals of the desert."

If we stick with the humanistic version of love, which is feeling and emotional-based reactions and acceptance. Then,

God would not make sense. Hate is the opposite of love, and if God can't deny Himself, then He can't hate, yet the Bible says he does. He must do one and not the other, which is true. However, when we recognize that love is a state of readiness, then it begins to make sense. Yet, for God, there is one more step to understanding His divine nature of love. God's love is the position of readiness, but it is a state of readiness that affirms and judges through His covenant. God's love is covenant-based. God's love and hate are not an emotional stance in any way but a positional stance on how God deals with you on a conventional level. This is how God loved David when he took Bathsheba away from Uriah the Hittite. He was unmistakably mad at David, and His anger burned hot at David's actions, so much so that God killed David's son born to her. This does not mean God's love (the covenant) broke off David. God has emotions just like He created us to have, and it is a fearful thing to fall into the hands of a wrathful God. However, God's love and hate have nothing to do with His emotions. God loved Jacob because he was God's chosen and hated Esau because He was placed outside of the covenant.

God's plan to execute His love in the world is to reach those who are lost souls. So much so that He was ready and willing to send Jesus His Son to die for them.

John 3:16 (ESV) - "For God so loved the world, that he gave his only Son, that whoever believes in him should not perish but have eternal life.

The love or readiness of God's favor is for those who choose Him in this life. For those who reject Him, He gives them to the devil. This does not mean that God stops chasing after them, but they are not His children. His beloved children are those who choose Him. These are those who follow Christ and accept God's love and law as a free gift. God longs for the lost to be saved, and as long as we draw breath, anyone can turn away from sin and change God's hate into love in their lives.

1 John 3:4-10 (ESV) - Everyone who makes a practice of sinning also practices lawlessness; sin is lawlessness. You know that he appeared in order to take away sins, and in him there is no sin. No one who abides in him keeps on sinning; no one who keeps on sinning has either seen him or known him. Little children, let no one deceive you. Whoever practices righteousness is righteous, as he is righteous. Whoever makes a practice of sinning is of the devil, for the devil has been sinning from the beginning. The reason the Son of God appeared was to destroy the works of the devil. No one born of God makes a practice of sinning, for God's seed abides in him; and he cannot keep on sinning, because he has been born of God. By this it is evident who are the children of God, and who are the children of the devil: whoever does not practice righteousness is not of God, nor is the one who does not love his brother.

What can Separate Us from God's Love?

The next verse I want to look at is one of the most misused scriptures in all of the Bible about love (Romans 8:35-39). People read these verses without understanding them because they heard them taught in the 3rd person as if God was speaking. When it is being spoken in the 1st person view of the author, they read them like God's love is keeping us bound to Himself. However, this verse has nothing to do with God's readiness to have us in covenant but what things in life are keeping us from the readiness to serve God.

Romans 8:35-39 (ESV) - Who shall separate **us** from the love of Christ? Shall tribulation, or distress, or persecution, or famine, or nakedness, or danger, or sword? As it is written, "For your sake we are being killed all the day long; we are regarded as sheep to be slaughtered." No, in all these things we are more than conquerors through him who loved us. For I am sure that neither death nor life, nor angels nor rulers, nor things present nor things to come, nor powers, nor height nor depth, nor anything else in all creation, will be able to separate us from the love of God in Christ Jesus our Lord.

These verses are powerful, but not in the sense that many use them. One easy way to get an easy understanding is to remove the "us" from verse 35, read it, and then add it back into it with the knowledge that it's not talking about just anyone. Instead, it's the disciples of Christ describing their love or readiness to serve Christ. They're saying that even if great suffering comes upon us, and not only if, but indeed, we have already suffered all these things. Nonetheless, we are still in love with Christ and the Father through Christ! People have tried everything to get us to deny Christ, even to the point of taking our lives. We are like *"Sheep to be slaughtered"*, but we will always be in a state of unwavering readiness to serve and build our relationship with God. If this were about God's love for us, then God would be the one suffering these things and staying faithful to us, which is ridiculous. God is always faithful; there is no denying that, but this verse is not about His love but the strength of our own love in the faith of adversity. We can love God because He first loved us. Then we can take the next step and say we can endure suffering and still reside in love because Christ did it first.

Jesus loved in the same way God loves, in the sense of being ready to serve in His ministry; Jesus was able to love as a human and in the covenant love of God. Jesus was both human and God at the same time, and in many aspects of who Jesus is physically, His life, and ministry, Jesus was exactly like us in every way. The exception to the rule is when the soul is the only key factor. The state of love comes directly from the soul. We talk about our actions coming from a soft or hard heart, but this is a figure of speech. Our fleshly heart only pumps blood around our bodies. What we are truly talking about is the working of the soul before the outward actions of our body go forth to do it. A hard heart will not be in a state of readiness, but a heart of flesh (Ezekiel 36:26) is in a state of love and ready to do the work. Flesh and blood are incapable of true love, but the love of oneself comes from our souls doing the work of God. Animals can be taught and trained to have reactions and desires, but unselfish love will always remain intangible to them. Animals' thoughts and desires will always revert to natural instincts when away from people for a long enough period of time. In comparison, human love is capable of remaining true in the lowest pits in the most persistent lonely times. This is because our image is in the form of God, not outwardly, but inwardly, and animal kind is created in natural thoughts alone. Animals' mindsets are temporary and worldly, and man's mindsets are set eternal and meant to be kingdom-based.

Jesus' compassion was for all men, yet His love (readiness to help) was set by the covenant He made with Abraham. This means His Earthly ministry was heavily centered around, but not limited to, Abraham's descendants. Israel is the one who alone bore the covenant of God, which is why we read passages like this:

Matthew 15:26-28 (KJV) - But he answered and said, It is not meet to take the children's bread, and to cast it to dogs. And she said, Truth, Lord: yet the dogs eat of the crumbs which fall from their masters' table. Then Jesus answered and said unto her, O woman, great is thy faith: be it unto thee even as thou wilt. And her daughter was made whole from that very hour.

Jesus came for Israel, His "firstborn son," and because He deals in covenant, that covenant was geared toward Israel; they are the true branches (Romans 11:16-24). So, when this woman came, she came as an outsider from the love that Jesus was purposed to do. But there is a qualification to this story. When we think about who belongs to God and how Israel began, we see that it started with Abraham, and because Abraham had faith in God, it was counted as righteousness. God accepts everyone who will have faith in Him, and even though God's covenant was for the people of Israel. Those who choose to have faith in God, just like this woman, will become graphed into the body of Christ. Israel may be the natural branches, but anyone who will put their faith in God will become part of the branches of God's family tree. It is through this faith that we become sons and daughters of God. Israel is a natural son, but through our faith, we become sons and daughters; we become part of the covenant as well and can partake in the love of God.

Chapter 9
Suffering

The question of suffering is probably the most concerning among believers. We all have seen friends, family, and innocent children get hurt in so many ways, and even when we pray, sometimes we don't seem to get the answers we are looking for. We believe that if we pray for child sex trafficking to come to a stop, then why does God not come and end it immediately? Many of us have heard the atheist arguments against God.

- **If God is all-powerful?**
- **And If God is all Loving?**
- **Why does evil and suffering exist?**

We have covered most of this already, so answering this should come easy. Yes, God is all-powerful, but we are also overseers of this world. We make it or break it by our deeds, hearts, and morals. The devil has as much power as we give to him in this world and our lives. The issue is most people are willing to give him that power by walking in sinful thoughts and deeds and turning their hearts from God. Next, it's a mistake to say that God is all loving, but rather, we should say God's nature is love. A state of readiness to draw us closer to Him or let us push Him away and bring the opposite effects of goodness onto ourselves. Furthermore, the first two points break down before we even get to the conclusion. The question of why evil and suffering exist will answer itself when we step back and understand the truth at each step.

In reality, there is no solution to suffering except for Jesus. In Jesus, we can find strength, peace, and hope, regardless if we get the answer of why. For Christians, suffering is not only something we go through but is a necessary part of our walk with God. Some suffering is evil; other times, suffering is from God. This means we need to come to understand when we should be battling suffering with every ounce of power within our being or recognize when God is using it to teach us and bring us closer to Him. I want to look at four different types of suffering we experience and how we should deal with it. One important note is that this is how to think about suffering logically. When people are in a current state of suffering, there is a time when logical thinking or answering the question of "why" is of no help to them. When people are in a state where they are searching for answers emotionally instead of logically, then the best answer we can give is to just be there for them. Hold them and let them know they are loved by us and God, and be there to help them. There will be time later to give logical answers to why, but this is not always the best thing to do in every situation.

1 – Suffering from Human Sin

It's no secret that humanity is in constant rebellion against God, and this will continue until after the 1,000-year reign. On that day, no one who opposes God will be left, but only His followers will remain. However, because throughout all of time, people have opposed God, they are doing the complete opposite will of the Father. This type of suffering does not have to come from a demonic force but can come from ourselves (Mankind). As fallen men and women, we can desire to pursue the passions of the flesh instead of God. We can only serve one thing, whether that is God, Satan, sin, or ourselves. We must choose who or what has the right to make the decisions in our lives (Matthew 6:24). While God is the focus of a person or situation, it brings the fruits of the spirit into the world.

Galatians 5:22-23 (NKJV) - But the fruit of the Spirit is love, joy, peace, longsuffering, kindness, goodness, faithfulness, gentleness, self-control. Against such there is no law.

This means opposing God or running the opposite way of the Father will bring to pass the direct opposite of the fruits of the spirit. These will be hate, sorrow, chaos, hostility, a will to harm, vileness, betrayal, hurt, and recklessness. All are leading to the idolatry of a demonic spirit or even putting ourselves into the role of God. The world wants to move as far away from God as possible, but when they do, they produce these things within themselves. Then, they want to blame God for the evil in the world. It is as if they dig a pit in the ground, blindfold themselves, and run into it, then blame God because they got hurt and are stuck in a pit. When God is entirely in charge of someone's life, it brings life and goodness to them and those around them. I encourage you to look at the lives of some of the genuinely godly men and women who have lived. You'll see that even in the most challenging times, they still produced the gifts of the spirit in their lives, and those around them have benefitted from the fruit. However, when God is pushed away, then death and destruction will ensue.

God has made it clear that He does not want these types of suffering to go on in the world. There will be trials and tests to grow us, but these should be met with growth and resilience, not harm and despair. Though, He also won't stop people from doing what they have in their hearts to do. This is where the gift of free will of God comes in. God has designed us to be free moral agents, and we have the choice to do good or evil. This is because, without free will, no true love exists. You can't force someone to love you; God will never do that. To reject God is not to say God will punish you because you choose not to love Him; rather, He gives you what you want and will cast you out eternally in the end and give you those desires of not wanting to be in His presence. Eternity is decided on Earth during our lives, and God will give us whatever eternity we choose through our faith and actions. That is true love, the freedom to push or pull from your desires. The problem is not with the choice itself but how blind people are to the truth that is before them. If people could see past their own desires and look for just one minute through the eyes of God, they could see what their choices in life would truly bring about.

With our inherited sinful nature, we have been mentally unplugged from God and plugged into the world. Being plugged into the world, we naturally neglect or fight God because of the battle between our flesh and soul. So many people choose the ways of the world, which will bring curses upon themselves and cause suffering for themselves and those around them. One of the apparent forms of suffering in America is our gluttony. We want to consume food that is too much or bad for us. This does not take a demonic spirit whispering in your ear; instead, it only takes a lack of self-control. When we eat like this, our bodies become the dwelling of suffering from our lack of self-control. The consequences of sin are lined out for us in the Bible, but we choose to ignore them.

James 1:14-15 (ESV) - But each person is tempted when he is lured and enticed by his own desire. Then desire when it has conceived gives birth to sin, and sin when it is fully grown brings forth death.

When we give into sin, suffering will always follow. Then, when we allow sin to be completed in our lives, it brings forth death. In Christ, death has no victory or sting. Outside of Christ, death becomes torment and will be victorious over the sinner.

Suffering is complex because there is always a line of choices people make to bring it to fulfillment. Sometimes, suffering does not even result from our actions but from others' sins. The story of Joseph is an excellent example of this. Even though Joseph didn't deserve jail, slavery, abandonment, or mistreatment, he received all these things. Still, God can take complex evil and suffering from others and work it out for Good (Genesis 50:20). The cross of Christ is the ultimate example of this (Romans 8:28, 1 Peter 2:21-25). We still may go through suffering because of others, but our goal is always Jesus, and He will tend to the endings.

2 - God Uses Suffering to Correct

If someone chooses to live in opposition to God, then God has choices to make as well. Sometimes, He chooses to have mercy and put suffering on us and around us so that He can save our souls. A good visual example of this would be during King Nebuchadnezzar's time as a wild animal to straighten out his thoughts and follow God rather than his own power.

1 Corinthians 5:5 (ASV) - to deliver such a one unto Satan for the destruction of the flesh, that the spirit may be saved in the day of the Lord Jesus.

Other times, when it's our flesh that is the problem and causing sin. He may also use us as an example so that others around us might be saved. Such would be of Pharoh's heart hardening and suffering so much loss, or those that oppose Arron high priest's position and the fire came from God and killed them. In Acts 5:1–11, a man named Ananias, along with his wife Sapphira, sold a piece of property. Then, they lied to the Apostles about their donation. God killed both of them so that the others would recognize the seditiousness of their spirits and that sin has no part in the church body. The friends and family of these two would experience the suffering of their passing. However, if they had chosen not to sin by lying, their family would not have had to endure the following suffering.

And you have forgotten the exhortation that addresses you as sons:
<u>*My son, do not take the Lord's discipline lightly*</u>
<u>*or lose heart when you are reproved by him,*</u>
<u>*for the Lord disciplines the one he loves*</u>
<u>*and punishes every son he receives.*</u>
<u>*Endure suffering as discipline:*</u>
God is dealing with you as sons. For what son is there that a father does not discipline? But if you are without discipline—which all receive—then you are illegitimate children and not sons. Furthermore, we had human fathers discipline us, and we respected them. Shouldn't we submit even more to the Father of spirits and live? For they disciplined us for a short time based on what seemed good to them, but he does it for our benefit, so that we can share his holiness. No discipline seems enjoyable at the time, but painful. Later on, however, it yields the peaceful fruit of righteousness to those who have been trained by it.
- Hebrews 12:5-11 (ESV)

Discipline, even painful discipline, is not bad when correctly handled by believers. In fact, we, as fallen Man, need it. When discipline is withheld, our hearts are susceptible to turning to evil through a lack of respect. The phrase, "spare the rod and spoil the child," is not a direct biblical quote and misses the importance of discipline that the Bible teaches us.

Proverbs 23:13-14 (KJV) - Withhold not correction from the child; For if thou beat him with the rod, he will not die. Thou shalt beat him with the rod, And shalt deliver his soul from Hell.

In order to be safe, whether as children or adults, we need to know the boundaries. Boundaries are able to keep us in our lane on the road of life. When we stop having respect for God or those around us, it becomes clearly evident. An early example of this is if an appropriately aged child is incapable of sitting and staying focused on something, then there is a great issue. We should be taught how to sit and meditate on the Lord even from a young age. If you have zero quiet time with God where you can be still and know that He is Lord, then evil will be knocking loudly on your door. This applies to children and adults. We need to have the forethought and self-will to sit with God without distraction or loss of focus. If you say that is impossible in your life or the life of your children, then you don't have God as your main priority in your life. Whatever your priority is in life, you will be willing to drop everything to go and do it. Frequently, we're busy like Martha, but as Jesus told her, the most important part is to sit still and listen at His feet. To be able to take in what he has for us in that moment.

God is our Father, and we will never outgrow or be mature enough to make our own choices without Him. When we become Christians, it is saying, God, I give you full control over myself, and you, O' God, are King. That means His word becomes an unbreakable law unto you. We live and die by the words of God, and when we neglect our citizenship of the Kingdom of Heaven, then the law will fall hard upon us, and we understand that we deserve the punishment, which is death. However, God is a merciful Lord and Savior who does not want to see us lost. God does everything in His power to bring us back into righteousness in Him. These things will not be pleasant or may even cause great pain, but they are necessary disciplines from the Lord to save our souls.

There are some that say God will never do anything to hurt us. However, those whose stories are told to us through the Bible would disagree heavily with that statement. Indeed, God will never do anything that will tempt you into going to hell. Nor will He cause us harm and take pleasure in doing it. Remember, He is a good father and only wants the best for us. A good father does not hold their child's hand and affirm them when they are trapped in sin. If a child is learning to drive a car and is on the wrong side of the road, a good father doesn't tell them it's okay because it makes them feel good. He takes action, such as grabbing the wheel, yelling at them, if he was able, he would even put down spikes on the wrong side of the road to make sure you stay in your lane. If the child is disobedient to all these, they will be made to walk until they can prove they are ready to try again responsibly.

God's dealings with us are 2-fold:

- **Judgment for actions.**
- **While dealing with our punishments, He makes a path for redemption.**

Many may not make the course correction to change and grab ahold of the truth in this life that God has for us. Often, this is due to their desires for evil exceeding the pain they can endure. God's desire for us is to live and live more abundantly. This includes not being held underwater by sin and drowning but learning how to break free and not making the same mistakes again. Growing to be stronger, keeping ourselves above the clutches of this world, and resisting the temptation of the enemy.

God does test us, but all temptations come from our fleshly desires and the principalities of darkness. As we have seen in Hebrews 12, God chastises those He loves. Our chastisements are punishments; through our narrow vision, punishments are never good. Nonetheless, we must remember that though they are never enjoyable, they are, in fact, good. When David took Bathsheba, God killed the son who was conceived through the act. When Moses hit the rock, God took away entering the promised land. When Miriam opposed Moses, she became a leper. In Mariam's case, God went further to explain why He was making her suffer.

But the LORD said to Moses, "If her father had but spit in her face, should she not be shamed seven days? Let her be shut outside the camp seven days, and after that, she may be brought in again." – Number 12:14 (ESV)

Today, we would liken the "spitting in your face" to getting a spanking from your dad in front of all your friends and sitting in the corner where they can see you wallowing in your punishment. However, that would not have been even close to the punishment that Mariam went through. Mariam went through God's punishment of leprosy; this painful suffering was for her to learn the lesson that God means what He says. He put Moses in charge and blessed Him. To oppose that command was to oppose God Himself. It shows contempt for God and that you believe your will is superior to God's in truth and decree. Being a Christian means sacrificing our flesh and accepting the Lord's will in our lives. When we choose to do our own will and follow what looks good to us, we are doing the exact same as Adam and Eve in the Garden.

Genesis 3:1-7 (ESV) -Now the serpent was more crafty than any other beast of the field that the Lord God had made. He said to the woman, "Did God actually say, 'You shall not eat of any tree in the garden'?" And the woman said to the serpent, "We may eat of the fruit of the trees in the garden, but God said, 'You shall not eat of the fruit of the tree that is in the midst of the garden, neither shall you touch it, lest you die.'" But the serpent said to the woman, "You will not surely die. For God knows that when you eat of it your eyes will be opened, and you will be like God, knowing good and evil." So, when the woman saw that the tree was good for food and that it was a delight to the eyes, and that the tree was to be desired to make one wise, she took of its fruit and ate, and she also gave some to her husband who was with her, and he ate. Then, the eyes of both were opened, and they knew that they were naked. And they sewed fig leaves together and made themselves loincloths.

What was Eve after when she ate the fruit? She wanted to eat the fruit regardless of the law. She wanted the creation but not the creator. When we reject God's law, we reject Him because we can't love Him without following the law (John 14:21). The world wants the good things, the beautiful, the pleasurable, the riches in life without the laws and judgments that the foundation of the earth was established upon. If we neglect the Word of God, the only result is that suffering will follow. Because of the choice Adam and Eve made by abandoning God's word, their life became void of God's presence and protection. They left peace and began to toil and suffer through the rest of their lives. Their actions caused a massive amount of suffering in their lives. Not only were they kicked out of Eden, but their son was murdered, and their other son became his murderer.

God warned them, yet they didn't listen, and even though Adam and Eve fell, God still made a way of redemption. For Adam and Eve, God made the first sacrifice, the killing and taking of innocent blood, to redeem those who were lost. For Cain, it was mercy so he could correct his life and start doing God's will to multiply over the face of the earth. I'm sure you have noticed in your own lives that there are no protocols for how God will deal with individuals when we sin and fall away from Him. God says,

"I will have mercy on whom I will have mercy, and I will have compassion on whom I will have compassion". - *Romans 9:15 (ESV)*

Some He will forgive and cause healing and restoration, such as the woman at the well. Others will bring great suffering of death upon themselves and those around them, such as Ananias and Sapphira, Sampson, or the pharaoh of Egypt.

So then it depends not on human will or exertion, but on God, who has mercy. - Romans 9:16 (ESV)

All we can do when we mess up is throw ourselves at the feet of Jesus and pray for mercy as King David did. He may give mercy, or He may not when it comes to the suffering in our lives. He is always merciful in forgiving our sins but not in negating the natural consequences of our actions. We can ask and wait to see what the Lord does. However, regardless of the mercy He may or may not show us, the Lord is always justified. It is never the righteous judge who is at fault but the criminal standing trial. No matter what, we need to get up, brush ourselves off, and continue in our walk and in our worship of our King.

What about challenging situations like concentration camps or child abuse? Why does God allow these things? The answer is three-fold.

- First, God allows our will to be done for good or evil. That is the only path that allows true love. Although there are some who choose to use that free will to cause harm and/or get temporary satisfaction in their flesh. If God did not allow evil, which is rebellion against Him, to happen, it would be the same as unnatural forced love.

- Second is the missed opportunities of God's people. For example, in the 1940s, there were 18,000 Protestant clergy members in Germany. About 3,000 supported Hitler, and about 3,000 opposed him. About 12,000 wanted to remain neutral. When he took office. Those who opposed Hitler died, and those who wished to remain neutral were forced to agree or die. What would be the difference if all of God's people had stood as one body of Christ and taken a stand? Most of the people of Germany were in the Church and could have been led to take that stand. However, when godly people don't stand for truth and righteousness, then evil will prevail. **God's people can't be bystanders or cowards in the nation's morality, or the principalities of darkness will consume it.**

- Third is the lack of God. If the Church is to stand for morality, it can't be part of the problem. The Church is to be the light of the world. This is impossible if it is filled with darkness. Our duties to God, ourselves, and the people of the world are to keep ourselves pure and be able to stand against the evils of the world. There were seven churches mentioned in Revelations. Most of them had issues, and they were inviting sinful things into their churches. The churches could no longer fight the sin they were accepting themselves. They had already lost the battle and were dead from the inside out.

The world can only change and become moral when truth and righteousness are in power, with Jesus as the focal point. Remove these things, and evil will be all we are left with.

3: Suffering is Used for Transformation, Growth, Identification, and the Kingdom's Progress

Sometimes, suffering happens when no one has done anything wrong. This is when God puts situations in place so that they will help us grow and change in the way He wants. God's goal is to save us, make us perfect, and have us working effectively for the kingdom of Heaven. It's sort of like this (a modern parable): the Kingdom of Heaven is like a fishing boat that went out to sea. On their voyage, they spot countless people drowning in the sea with no means to be saved. There had been a shipwreck earlier because the captain of the other ship did not hold the course and crashed into rocks along the way. Many in the captain's crew knew about the rocks and did nothing to change course. Many on the sunken ship had no idea of why their ship sank at all. The captain of the fishing boat ordered the crew to rescue those in the water, so they started throwing out life-saving devices. However, many of the people in the water looked at the captain and did not like how He was calling out orders to grab the devices thrown at them. Many of these refused to be saved, waiting in the water until the sea swallowed them up. Some decided to make it to land by swimming on their own, but all of them were lost as well. Finally, there were those who followed the captain's orders to grab the life-saving devices. All those who were pulled onto the fishing boat and rescued were given new clothes, and they were able to aid in the rescue of the others in the water themselves.

In this parable, there were those on a ship who were enjoying themselves but had to put everything aside to focus on the task at hand, which was saving the lost. There were those in the water for no fault of their own. Then there are those in the water who were at fault and had to choose to be saved and face the consequences of their past actions or remain lost. In all these situations, no matter if you were safe on the boat or floundering in the water, they were all in a state of suffering. Even those on the boat had to give up their plans and start working for other people's sake. Nonetheless, For those on the boat, there was no fear of drowning because their feet were planted on the deck of the ship. They were safe, though they could not just enjoy their trip, they were working to save lives. Christians who grow through struggles and suffering can always have the confidence that no matter what, they are safe, and even if they perish from this life, they will awaken in Glory. Even physical death has no victory over them. It can only deliver them to their Lord.

Why does God allow suffering at all? Why can't we just be happy and pain-free our whole lives? I would like you, as a Christian, to think about that for a moment. What would your personal life be like if you could be pain-free and guaranteed not to be able to die? Even for a short time, What if no one could have an injury or die until the age of 50? How would you act? Would you rely on the Lord as much as you do now? Would you pray at all? Now, think about the world, the lost world around you, if no one had to fear death or pain. Would it be a beautiful world? Would the major events around us, such as world wars, terrorist attacks, or disasters, be greater or less? Every time one of these events takes place, church attendance goes way up. People flock to a place where they think they can receive peace and comfort in hard times. God speaks loudest to us when we are feeling pain. Pain can get our attention and make us re-evaluate what is going on. In reality, God is not speaking any louder, but we are definitely listening harder.

God does not like to see suffering, but it is a tool to get people or nations' attention. When a child is young and sees fire and wants to play with it. As a parent, you might tell them a hundred times that it's not safe, but one time of getting burned will cement the realization into their minds forever. It does not even have to be something sinful. We learn many things, especially as children, that hurt when we fail, such as falling when climbing trees or riding a horse. We are supposed to use that time to learn how to get better and grow so that next time, we don't have to feel the pain or at least reduce it. If we are doing something repeatedly and suffering for it more and more, then there is probably an issue with what we are participating in. Examples would be sex outside of marriage, drug use, tobacco, or alcohol. These things stimulate your brain and emotions at first and then lead to destruction and death. They grow in suffering and tear apart the one who does them.

When pain occurs, we understand that there is something wrong, and through pain, we know that there must be a change of some kind. God often uses this to get our attention; He says I need you to learn, change, and grow stronger.

James 1:2-4 (NKJV) - My brethren, count it all joy when you fall into various trials, knowing that the testing of your faith produces patience. But let patience have its perfect work, that you may be perfect and complete, lacking nothing.

We don't have to be in sin to go through suffering, but through suffering, we can learn to be reliant on the Lord. We can look at Job's struggles. Job was righteous, but God allowed struggle and great suffering to prove his loyalty to God. Though in obvious agony, Job always leaned farther into the Lord and didn't pull away. Through all his problems, Job was rewarded for his faithfulness in the end. God does let us go through trials, and it's through these trials that the Lord wants us to lean into Him and grow stronger.

God does not want weak Christians; We are fighting a spiritual battle, not against flesh and blood but against spiritual enemies (Ephesians 6:12). There is a reason why the US military forces have boot camps and training. If you have experienced these yourself or know people who have been through this training. Then you know it is not pleasant, and a lot of suffering goes on. However, it is not suffering to tear you down but to equip the men and women to handle situations and be able to fight the opposition they will face during battle.

1 Peter 5:10 (ESV) - And after you have suffered a little while, the God of all grace, who has called you to his eternal glory in Christ, will himself restore, confirm, strengthen, and establish you.

God does that for His people as well. It is better for you to be able to grow stronger so you can fight better. We must go through things to be able to win battles later on. Knowing that training comes with suffering, there are many that go into the training camp ready to be built up. While others will be scared away in fear of the pain. For the Christian, suffering is meant to equip you. It's not a problem or hurdle for you to fall over, but the spiritual gym so that whatever comes after will seem easy. Not only because you are spiritually stronger but also because during your hard times, you leaned into the Lord and grew closer to Him each step of the way. No matter how strong we might become, our closeness with God will always be our core strength and shield.

Isaiah 30:20-21(ESV) - And though the Lord give you the bread of adversity and the water of affliction, yet your Teacher will not hide himself anymore, but your eyes shall see your Teacher. And your ears shall hear a word behind you, saying, "This is the way, walk in it," when you turn to the right or when you turn to the left.

The last part of this is to keep in mind that we are not the main characters of this story. This world and its story are about Jesus and the Kingdom of Heaven. We often look at our lives and wonder why we have to go through this. We forget that all things are to work for the good of our Lord. We might have to put up with some suffering, perhaps for a good part of our lives, but if it means that God can use us to show the world a little more about Himself, then God be the glory.

John 9:1-3 (NKJV) - Now as Jesus passed by, He saw a man who was blind from birth. And His disciples asked Him, saying, "Rabbi, who sinned, this man or his parents, that he was born blind?" Jesus answered, "Neither this man nor his parents sinned, but that the works of God should be revealed in him.

This adult man was blind from birth so that one day, Jesus could come and heal him. This was a testimony to all who saw it and a lesson for those who were blind spiritually. God had a purpose and plan for this man's life and for this point in time when they were to meet. We all have a part in God's plan, and only He knows the outcome of all the situations and trials that we will face. Maybe it is to be a Paul and to be a witness to the world, or maybe it is to be used as an example of God's power. No matter what God has planned for us, our job is to be obedient and follow Him every day.

One thing we can't do in life is hold resentment for the suffering that we go through. We need to use each situation to grow stronger and grow closer to God. This is one thing that Cain missed. God spoke openly to Cain and gave him a warning.

Genesis 4:7 (NKJV) - If you do well, will you not be accepted? And if you do not do well, sin lies at the door. And its desire is for you, but you should rule over it."

When we go through suffering and hold resentment in our hearts, it will pull us far away from the Lord. Our life will include suffering; the rain falls of the just and unjust; no matter if we are saints or sinners. Yet more than that, suffering is what corrects and builds us up to be strong Christians and people in general. Know that God plans to use you on the battlefield, and if you are ready, you can survive the most significant battles and be an overcomer. Even if this temporal life passes away, we still win. Many times, we can't see or understand the why. We can know and trust the one in control and lean into the Father.

Romans 5:3-5 (ESV) - Not only that, but we rejoice in our sufferings, knowing that suffering produces endurance, and endurance produces character, and character produces hope, and hope does not put us to shame, because God's love has been poured into our hearts through the Holy Spirit who has been given to us.

4: Suffering is a Reminder of God's Love, Grace, and Presence

When I was a child, I spoke like a child, I thought like a child, I reasoned like a child. When I became a man, I gave up childish ways. - 1 Corinthians 13:11 (ESV)

We think we know everything growing up until we come to the realization that there is so much more we don't know compared to our current knowledge. This is and will be the case throughout our entire lives. As you have gone through this book, I hope you found a few things that were new to you or different from what you believed to be accurate. That is a good thing; we need to be able to test our knowledge and grow by learning new knowledge and implementing those things into our lives. That is what it means to continue to grow in Christ.

Growing up, we find ourselves under the authority of our parents or guardians. If you think back, you'll probably remember times that upset you because you didn't get your way. Whether it was eating too many sweets or they were against you dating a particular individual. We don't understand these things in our adolescence, and how too much candy could hurt you. Perhaps you didn't realize how the person you like could possibly be wrong for you. However, as we grow older, we can understand where our parents came from. We can appreciate that they didn't let us make all the wrong choices and how they corrected us when we made them. God does this for us now as well. God is the supreme and mature authority, and in the same way, our parents were the mature authorities in our lives as children. He is correcting us because we are heading for trouble and wants to ensure we stay out of harm's way. It may feel like suffering now, but He only tries to keep us from real suffering and eternal damnation.

No matter what we go through in this life, we should be reminded that when we face suffering, we know God is with us and for us. When Israel was disobedient to God, He sent snakes among the people. The snakes caused great suffering and pain, and the pain was a reminder and punishment for their actions. However, God decided to deal with the people differently than usual. He had Moses make a serpent and lift it on a pole. People could look at the serpent and be healed. This was God's mercy; they could not escape what they had done, but through their pain and God's plan, they could find peace and healing. They had to acknowledge that the image was a visual example of their sin. This was an image of Christ being lifted for our sins. We can turn to Christ for forgiveness and healing. Christ wants us to be healed and for suffering to end in our lives, but more than that, He wants us to purge all sinfulness out of our lives. Jesus wants to walk with us and be the healing and strength we need to get through each situation.

We don't have a lot of choices regarding what happens to us, especially when it is outside of our control. Such as a nation at war, Christian persecution, or sickness; the list is almost endless. However, no matter the situation, Jesus is always the answer. He can carry us through and give us strength physically and spiritually. He alone can be our Savior. As Christians, we should not only endure suffering but also be glad when we can go through it. Praising the Lord along the way, so that the world can see how our God helps us overcome all things.

2 Corinthians 12:9-10 (NKJV) - And He said to me, "My grace is sufficient for you, for My strength is made perfect in weakness." Therefore most gladly I will rather boast in my infirmities, that the power of Christ may rest upon me. Therefore I take pleasure in infirmities, in reproaches, in needs, in persecutions, in distresses, for Christ's sake. For when I am weak, then I am strong.

Through all of this, Jesus' goal is not for us to have to run to Him in troubled times. Instead, Jesus' goal is that we remain in Him, and when trials come, we are already strong enough, comforted enough, and continually reside in the hope and peace of our Christ. He wants us to be like a house built upon the rock prepared before the storms come (Matthew 7:24-29). Sadly, this is often not where we find ourselves. Many run to God after the storm starts, and maybe we get through it, but then shortly after forget Him when things level out. God wants continual growth and strengthening in each son or daughter. If trials come, our Lord always wants us to recognize Him as our savior, strength, and firm foundation. Even when He puts trials upon you to get you back to the place you need to be, remember that He is the point of restoration and healing for each and everything we face.

Lamentations 3:22-23 (ESV) - The steadfast love of the Lord never ceases; his mercies never come to an end; they are new every morning; great is your faithfulness.

Conclusion of Suffering

We all seek proof in our lives. We seek out the rationale and go with what we know to be the best answers. The most important thing we know about suffering is that it is a part of life. No one can escape or avoid it, but we can find the best way to cope with it, and that is Jesus. Jesus gave all He had, even His life, to show you how to deal with suffering. He endured more suffering than anyone who has walked on the earth to let you know that you can do it, too. Jesus is not asking you to do anything he has not already done, but He tells us that He will be with us through the thick and thin and see us through until the end. All we must do is believe, trust in Jesus, and follow His example.

1 Peter 2:21-25 (ESV) - For you have been called for this purpose, because Christ also suffered for you, leaving you an example, so that you would follow in His steps, He who committed no sin, nor was any deceit found in His mouth; and while being abusively insulted, He did not insult in return; while suffering, He did not threaten, but kept entrusting Himself to Him who judges righteously; and He Himself brought our sins in His body up on the cross so that we might die to sin and live for righteousness; by His wounds you were healed. For you were continually straying like sheep, but now you have returned to the Shepherd and Guardian of your souls.

Chapter 10
The Power of the Christian

Where does our strength come from?

Psalm 28:7 (KJV) - The LORD is my strength and my shield; my heart trusted in him, and I am helped: therefore my heart greatly rejoiceth; and with my song will I praise him.

Our strength comes from letting go and letting God move in our lives. The more we let go of relying on our own strength, our own desires, and our own ability to accomplish things in our lives, the more we will be able to achieve. Only one of the two entities has the ability to work in the Christian life: God or ourselves. We can move, or God can move through us. When we rely on God and His will, He can work powerfully in our lives through the Holy Spirit, but why? Why is the power of God able to move through people in mighty ways?

"And Jesus said unto them, Because of your unbelief: for verily I say unto you, If ye have faith as a grain of mustard seed, ye shall say unto this mountain, Remove hence to yonder place; and it shall remove, and nothing shall be impossible unto you." Matthew 17:20 (KJV)

- What gives a Christian this kind of power in this world?
- Why does it seem so hard for us to be able to attain it?

The answer to the first question should give us faith, and the answer to the second question will let us know how to attain the power promised to us.

What Gives Christians Power in this World?

The Universe is not what it appears to be, and science is just now coming to that realization. Let's dive into the intriguing world of modern fundamental physics. At the tiniest scales, nothing is truly solid, as we commonly think of things being physical. Instead, we encounter only energy packets, tiny building blocks that can behave both like waves and particles. Some of these particles have mass but are only bonded and twisted energy, constituting our idea of matter, while others lack mass; they're known as radiation or force carriers. However, they're all different forms of the same underlying thing: energy. Surprisingly, particles with mass can transform into massless particles and vice versa. Mass becomes a transitory property, appearing and disappearing, while the total energy remains constant. God has designed our universe to maintain the same amount of energy where it can't be gained or lost unless the change comes from Him. When we observe these subatomic entities, we don't see solid balls; instead, we catch glimpses of energy packets concentrated at specific points in space and time. Their behavior defies what many would call common sense. They can't be straightforward particles following predictable paths. Instead, they act like waves, leading us to a cosmic conundrum. Our reality is a mix of particles that we interact with on a daily basis and an unseen wave-based world described only by theory in the scientific world.

The problem science has and will always have is that it has the wrong starting point. All waves carry information; even our voices make pressure waves of data in the air that our God-given brains can decode and help us perceive the world around us. All of creation is waves of data; as God speaks, He forces energy into our plane of existence. His voice forms the data of the energy waves into what we perceive as reality. His voice controls the binding and releasing of the energy waves, making and unmaking our physical plane of existence. Scientists are trying to theorize what other universes or planes of existence are out there that can make this work. Nevertheless, God has already revealed all this in His word from the very start. God is the programmer, designer, and power source of this world. The waves of the ultimate eternal being, the I AM, who spoke, and we came forth. This is known to Christians as the voice of the Lord.

As God spoke, the material world came into being through His creative power. God did not command spiritual workers to start building the world one particle at a time, like tiny building blocks. Instead, by the power of His mouth alone, He created everything. As He spoke the words, energy came from His mouth, and bond particles of the sun and moon came into existence. The fabric of reality bent to the creator's will and produced from nothing but the energy of His breath and the data it contained by His words, the very existence of these two celestial objects. Think about the programmer mentioned before in other chapters; God (the programmer) is writing the code, and the object is created inside His program. One moment, there is nothing, and then He writes the code, and it appears: God's voice controls the universe. His speech is the programming, and through His unlimited power, those things come into being.

Psalms 29:1-11 (ESV) - Ascribe to the Lord, O heavenly beings, ascribe to the Lord glory and strength. Ascribe to the Lord the glory due his name; worship the Lord in the splendor of holiness. The voice of the Lord is over the waters; the God of glory thunders, the Lord, over many waters. The voice of the Lord is powerful; the voice of the Lord is full of majesty. The voice of the Lord breaks the cedars; the Lord breaks the cedars of Lebanon. He makes Lebanon to skip like a calf, and Sirion like a young wild ox. The voice of the Lord flashes forth flames of fire. The voice of the Lord shakes the wilderness; the Lord shakes the wilderness of Kadesh. The voice of the Lord makes the deer give birth and strips the forests bare, and in his temple all cry, "Glory!" The Lord sits enthroned over the flood; the Lord sits enthroned as king forever. May the Lord give strength to his people! May the Lord bless his people with peace!

Only one thing is not part of this material creation but remains part of our world. Something that does not come from the spoken words of God nor contain the same energy that constitutes all of what we can understand as the matter and energy around us. This mysterious thing is the human soul. The human soul was not spoken into creation. The human body was formed from the dust of the ground, which is part of our existence, but the living soul was breathed into man after he was formed.

Genesis 2:7 (KJV) - And the LORD God formed man of the dust of the ground, and breathed into his nostrils the breath of life and man became a living soul.

All other parts of His creation were forced into existence by the direction of His voice. Nevertheless, the breath of life was put into Man directly. This makes our soul different in form and type than all things created and remaining in the existence that is around us. One reason we cannot find or study the human soul is that we are only able to detect and study the forms of energy that make up our plane of existence. However, all things that don't share the same type of energy, souls, angles, and all spiritual existence, such as angel chariots, are not detectable to any human equipment that relies on our own form of energy to understand the things around it. At times, the spiritual plane shows itself to us, and we can see and interact with them at their inclination. Since our souls are created with the same energy that exists from the spiritual plane of existence. It helps us understand why when all physical existence is melted away in the last days only the human souls remain standing in front of God for the Great White Throne Judgement.

If God is the programmer of this world, how does this apply to Christians? How can a believer tell a mountain to move, and it picks itself up and will be tossed into the sea? The answer rests in the Trinity. The Father, Son, and Holy Spirit are all God; all are creators and programmers of this universe. Any of them can call the sun, moon, and stars into existence with the words from their mouths and have the power to bring them into existence. When Jesus was done with His mission and before He ascended, He told us He would send the comforter to us.

John 14:16-18 (ASV) - And I will pray the Father, and he shall give you another Comforter, that he may be with you for ever, even the Spirit of truth: whom the world cannot receive; for it beholdeth him not, neither knoweth him: ye know him; for he abideth with you, and shall be in you. I will not leave you desolate: I come unto you.

John 14:26 (ASV) - But the Comforter, even the Holy Spirit, whom the Father will send in my name, he shall teach you all things, and bring to your remembrance all that I said unto you.

The Holy Spirit, who is part of the Trinity and has all power over life and death, creation and destruction, has come to us and lives in the people of God. Not only does He live in us, but he empowers the believers. Then, we can align ourselves to the same position that the Holy Spirit is in, and He is free to use us to do His will. Our mouths can speak and cause the healing of others, mountains to move, walls to crumble, and the very gates of hell to shake and fall to our feet. Literally, the same power that can create the universe by the waves and energy of God's voice can come from our lips. Solomon spoke wisely when he said:

Proverbs 18:21 (KJV) - Death and life are in the power of the tongue: and they that love it shall eat the fruit thereof.

The problem that most people have is the alignment that it takes for the Holy Spirit to move through us. In most things that God does in the world, He does through those who love and follow after Him. The entire Bible is filled with stories about people doing mighty things through the power that God uses through them. God's power is not something we can take by force to fulfill our wants or desires. Rather, to perform miracles and do what seems impossible, like moving a mountain, we must find ultimate submission. We must release things from ourselves and become willing vessels to God's desires. This seems impossible at first, but the more you free yourself from the world, the more your desire will align with God's. Once we get to this place, we will find that you and your Lord have become so intimate that when He speaks, you speak; when He moves, you move. This is how we can finally get to the place where we are doing greater works than He did.

Why it Seems Hard for Us to Attain It?

1 - Be Like Christ

Often, we get in the way. We ask God in the wrong way and for the wrong reasons.

James 4:3 (ASV) - Ye ask, and receive not, because ye ask amiss, that ye may spend it in your pleasures.

The truth today about what it means to be a Christian is often ridiculed because it takes too much work to accomplish. The word Christian literally translates to "little anointed ones." Christ was the Anointed One, so we are to be little Christs. When people evaluate our lives, they should see that there was a point when you looked like the world in every way, and then you changed to look like Jesus.

Romans 13:14 (ASV) - But put on the Lord Jesus Christ, and make no provision for the flesh, to gratify its desires.

The first step in attaining the power Jesus granted us is putting on Christ. Jesus never intended for anyone to represent Him in word or power if they are not examples of Himself. This first requires us to understand who He is and then make the necessary changes to conform to His standards of living and morality. We know that He is not only willing for us to do great works in His name but also longs for it.

John 14:12 (KJV) - Verily, verily, I say unto you, He that believeth on me, the works that I do shall he do also; and greater works than these shall he do; because I go unto my Father.

Jesus sent the Holy Spirit to us not only to benefit us in our walk but also so that we could do great works in His name. The Church working in this way is part of the Lord's plan, and if He wants it to be done, then He will give us the way and power to accomplish it.

James 4:15 (ASV) - For that ye ought to say, If the Lord will, we shall both live, and do this or that.

John 9:4-5 (ASV) - We must work the works of him that sent me, while it is day: the night cometh, when no man can work. When I am in the world, I am the light of the world.

Often, we think about this verse as talking about ministry, which it is in part. However, when we read this carefully, We notice in verse 5 that He is talking about the Church having a job to do before the rapture of the Church. When the Church is pulled off the Earth, and the bridegroom is gone to the Marriage Supper of the Lamb, the power of the Church that is allowed by God will be gone as well. People will still be able to find forgiveness and even die for their faith during the tribulation. This means something besides salvation is being described here. What Jesus is telling us here is that the power we have through the Holy Spirit and His mission here on Earth will be gone. Therefore, use it while you can. Jesus is reminding us that the power bestowed on the Church is meant to be used in even bigger ways than Jesus used in His ministry to reach the lost. In fact, when we read the context associated with John 9:1- 7, it is Jesus healing the man born blind from birth. When He says these words, He is doing an impossible feat of healing and telling us to do the same.

2 – Sanctification Not for Self-Glorification

When healing and miracles occur, people come running, trying to find out what is going on and how they can be part of it. Jesus reminds us that these miracles are for us to do and are something we ought to be doing to move the Kingdom of God forward. It is never about us showing off or getting the power to use at our whim. It is not a superpower you receive by getting bit by the Holy Spirit. It is you giving yourself to God to be used and God using you in the way that He sees fit. In the Bible, we have 2 verses that show both intentions of people.

James 5:16 (ASV) - Confess therefore your sins one to another, and pray one for another, that ye may be healed. The supplication of a righteous man availeth much in its working.

VS.

Acts 8:17-24 (ASV) - .... Now when Simon saw that through the laying on of the apostles' hands the Holy Spirit was given, he offered them money, saying, Give me also this power, that on whomsoever I lay my hands, he may receive the Holy Spirit. But Peter said unto him, Thy silver perish with thee, because thou hast thought to obtain the gift of God with money.....

Simon the sorcerer wanted to edify himself and thought there was another way of receiving the power of the Holy Spirit other than submission. This is a direct blasphemy of the Holy Spirit. The Holy Spirit, being God, cannot be bought, used, or forced to do anything outside of His own will. Rather, if we want to be used by the Holy Spirit, James 5:16 is clear. We need to sanctify ourselves and live righteously before the Lord. Then, as a righteous man, we can be a great vessel to do the Lord's will. If we are living a life that is filled with continual sin, then our vessel is dirty or broken and cannot be used.

2 Timothy 2:1–26 (ESV) - ....Now in a great house there are not only vessels of gold and silver but also of wood and clay, some for honorable use, some for dishonorable. Therefore, if anyone cleanses himself from what is dishonorable, he will be a vessel for honorable use, set apart as holy, useful to the master of the house, ready for every good work....

God can use everyone, but for those who want to see the full power of the Kingdom of God used in their life and be a vessel of honor, it takes us being clean. In the world today, many preachers stand at the pulpit and tell you that you are just a sinful man and that you will fail every day. This is wrong on so many levels. If you are sinning every day, then you need to take a step back and evaluate what is going on. There are areas in your life that need to be cut out and tossed aside so that you can live Godly lives, honoring and respecting the Father in Heaven. Jesus' call is to be perfect as He is perfect, and being lazy and sinful does dishonor to our Lord and Savior. Not only as our Father who created us but also as a Savior who died so you can have life and life more abundantly. God can use anyone He wishes; He can use Balaam to bless the people, Sampson to kill His enemy, or Rahab to help defeat a city. There is always a point where God will stop using us, or if He uses the wicked to accomplish His goals, then punishment will follow, such as Nebuchadnezzar.

This also doesn't mean that we can't fail if we do our best. Peter had to be rebuked by Paul because of His actions (Galatians 2:11-14). However, if we fall, we learn how to humble ourselves, turn from evil, and flow back into the righteousness and sanctification found in Jesus and follow His way. Until our last breath, there is always hope in the Lord, and even the worst of the worst in the world can find and serve God as a vessel of Gold if they will only fully submit to Him.

Faith of a Mustard Seed

We do not need to define ourselves or wonder about faith because it is clearly defined in God's Word. We Hope for the things not seen, with the assurance of evidence of who we know God to be. The verses that follow the book of Hebrews show us many examples of faith. In each case, they lived out their faith, believing what they could not see but having full assurance that it was the only actual reality.

Hebrews 11:1 (NKJV) - Now faith is the substance of things hoped for, the evidence of things not seen.

To better understand faith, envision someone shooting a bow and arrow. When you shoot a bow, you can place an arrow on the string. Draw back the bow and sight in your target. Then release the arrow and allow what happens naturally to take place. There is a right way and a wrong way to shoot a bow. No one puts an arrow on a string, pulls it back, and then takes it off the string, running up to the target and pushing it in with your hands. Instead, you must have trust in your bow, arrow, physics, and skills to know that you will hit what you are aiming at. There can be many things that affect your shot. Maybe you pulled your wrist in anticipation of the release. Maybe a gust of wind will blow the arrow off course. Perhaps you missed a step when lining up your shot or did not calculate the distance the arrow would have to travel. There are many variables; however, if you take time and practice, you can have confidence that when you shoot, you can hit the target every time. We can do things that mess up the shot, but if we get everything right, we know that we won't miss what we are aiming at. God never allows us to shoot our arrows point blank or to take them off the string and place them in the target. God always has us put in time, practice, and test our endurance and trust that when we step out in faith, God will not let us fall. When you look at the prophets of old or the apostles, they had complete faith that their words would come to pass. We can do the same things through the same power of the Holy Spirit *(Matthew 17:20)*.

For those who will boldly approach the throne, who are willing to set aside all their fleshly desires and become one in mind with God, let God sanctify you and drive you as a captain at the helm of your life. For those people, you can step out in your faith and take your shot trusting in the Lord. Then, through the power of the Holy Spirit in you, you will remove mountains from their location and see many mighty works being done through you. These things are not done by any power of ourselves, but if we are willing vessels of honor, God will use us. He patiently waits for those special people to say yes to Him. For many people today, there is not enough trust in God to even put the arrow on the string, let alone take a shot of faith in a situation.

Even though God can use us to do all these things through our faith, it is not the most important thing we must dwell on. **The most essential thing in our lives is that our names are written down in the Lamb's Book of Life.** To be the Bride of Christ and eagerly expecting the Lord's return is the thought that consumes us. God bless you, and Godspeed in all your work for the Lord.

Shalom, Shalom.

Acknowledgements:

Scripture quotations marked (ESV) are from the English Standard Version of the Bible: The ESV Global Study Bible®, ESV® Bible, Copyright © 2012 by Crossway. All rights reserved.
The Holy Bible, English Standard Version® (ESV®) © 2001 by Crossway, a publishing ministry of Good News Publishers.

Scripture quotations marked (KJV) are from the King James Version of the Bible: the KJV is in the public domain, and there are no restrictions. However, in the UK, the translation is owned by the Crown and published by Cambridge, and there are restrictions and notification rules similar to those for other translations.

Scripture quotations marked (NKJV) are from the King James Version of the Bible: "Scripture taken from the New King James Version. Copyright © 1982 by Thomas Nelson, Inc. Used by permission. All rights reserved."

Scripture quotations marked (ASV) are from American Standard Bible.
The American Standard Version entered the public domain on January 1, 1957 upon expiration of its copyright. The American Standard Version (ASV) came into being due to the leadership of Phillip Schaff, who assembled a team comprised of 30 American and British scholars. Work on the ASV was completed in 1901. The translation was tasked with the goal of an accurate, literal, word-for-word translation of the Holy Scriptures.

Made in the USA
Columbia, SC
24 October 2024

44630133R00085